PSALMS

to Accompany the Spiritual Exercises of St Ignatius Loyola

PSALMS

to Accompany the
Spiritual Exercises of
St Ignatius Loyola

by

Benjamín González Buelta SJ

translated from the Spanish by
Damian A. Howard SJ

© The Way
First published 2012 by
Way Books, Campion Hall,
Oxford, OX1 1QS
www.theway.org.uk

Original Spanish edition *Salmos para gustar y sentir
internamente* © Editorial Sal Terrae 2004
We are grateful for permission to publish this translation.

Cover design: Peter Brook SJ
Cover photograph © Urs Hauenstein,
www.picsfrom.com

British Library Cataloguing-in-Publication Data
A catalogue record for this book is available from the
British Library

ISBN 978 0 904717 40 2

CONTENTS

PROLOGUE

The people of Israel exceeded the achievements of all the other nations in the arts of poetry and lyrics. In the literary genre of the hymn, they found the means to invoke and sing directly to their God, thus expressing poetically their love and praise. In the multicoloured patchwork that makes up the text of the Bible, we find, mixed in with prophetic, normative and narrative writings, the religious poetry of the chosen people, filling the pages of scripture with beauty and expressing in an unequalled manner the love of the people for their God.

So the Psalms are sacred hymns through which the people of God used to praise the Most High, beseeching His mercy, thanking Him for gifts received and recording the mighty works of His father-like providence for Israel. They were put together from various sacred writings, most of them attributed to King David. The Hebrews called these songs *thehillim* (hymns), later to be known as *salmos*, as they were sung to the sound of an instrument that the Greeks called the *salterio*.

All pious Jews made the Psalms their particular way of praying. We can imagine Joseph, Mary and Jesus praying these songs as poems handed down by their ancestors. Written before the coming of Jesus, prayed and sung by him at key moments of his life, including the passion, the Psalms were part of the heritage left by the messiah to those who would make up his Church, the community of the new covenant, the new people of God.

Throughout the 2,000-year history of Christianity, women and men, moved and inspired by the Spirit of God, have expressed and invoked the One for whom their hearts yearned using the poetic literary style of the Psalms. These poems, songs and hymns of praise, petition, penitence and joy, always had two purposes: to express the believer's feelings of faith, love and reverence, and to help others to experience and express those same feelings. The experience of the psalmist seeks out the heart of another praying person, offering a way and a manner to speak and to name the One who fills his or her heart.

This book follows the same pattern. Benjamín González Buelta is a Spanish Jesuit who, for over forty years, has been living in Central America and the Caribbean. Of his thirty-seven years in the Dominican Republic, he was Master of Novices for seventeen and Provincial for six. Currently he is Regional Superior of Cuba. His life has always been marked—whether as *formatore* or superior—by the Spiritual Exercises of Ignatius of Loyola. These give structure to his

Jesuit life and he tries to impart them to others, Jesuits and lay people, religious, priests, bishops—in sum, to the whole range of people who come to him seeking to nourish their experience of God.

Giving the Exercises to all sorts of people over the years, Benjamín sensed that he could put his God-given gift of poetry at the service of this ministry. The psalms that he wrote out of his own prayer could be used by those making the Exercises to help them overcome any difficulties that they might have with the harshness of Ignatius' own language or with some experience that they were seeking without managing to find.

The author sensed that his psalms, born of his own experience of God, were looking for similar experiences, lived or desired by those making the Exercises. Retreatants, in their turn, through the inspired simplicity of the poet's verses, could move forward, finding a way of entering more deeply into the process and pedagogy of Ignatius. A collection of Benjamín's psalms was finally published in Havana in 2002. The current volume is a translation of that Havana selection, supplemented by other psalms which struck us as suited to the author's intention: that of accompanying the Spiritual Exercises.

Benjamín's poetry uses certain leitmotifs which lend it its originality: his profound sense of the beauty of creation; his tender love for people; and his acute sensitivity to injustice, oppression and social sin. However, it is not so much his own way of thinking that he desires to pass on through his psalms. More than anything else, what he is trying to do is to open a path so that through their own experiences others can discover and experience the God who speaks to them and desires passionately to reveal Himself through the beauty of creation, in the tenderness of feelings and loving relationships, and in the indignation and pain of sacrificing one's own life without recompense when faced with injustice and the suffering of others. He puts his experience at the service of his readers so as to support them on a journey—as an older, more experienced brother—which has been trodden since time immemorial.

This is why each psalm is introduced by a quotation from the *Spiritual Exercises*, so that readers who are making the Exercises can more easily find the passage to which it refers or might refer, thus naming their experience and the movement of their heart. The psalms are divided according to the stages of the Exercises. But before tackling the First Principle and Foundation, which forms the gateway to them, we have included some psalms that will help those making the Exercises tune in to God's wavelength and dispose themselves to the experience that God seeks to give them.

We hope that this little psalter may be as useful to the director as to the retreatant. The great French philologist Roland Barthes wrote a memorable study in which he identifies four textual levels in the *Spiritual Exercises*: i) that which God wrote in the life and experience of Ignatius; ii) that which Ignatius wrote and committed to the book of the *Exercises*; iii) that which the director 'writes' in the direction he or she gives to the retreatant; iv) the final text which is the objective of this series of human and divine revelations, none other than the text that God and the retreatant, burning and locked in embrace (see Annotation 15), write together in loving communion, renewing once more in history the marvel of the Spirit that makes all things new.

The psalms of Benjamín González Buelta are situated between the third and fourth levels. On the one hand, they help the director to open up new possibilities for the retreatant in accessing the Ignatian Exercises with words and experience that follow Ignatius in creative fidelity. On the other hand, they allow the same retreatant, moved by the Spirit towards discipleship of Christ and the will of the Father, inspired and held by love, to write his or her own psalms of praise, helping that person to live totally turned towards the reverence and service of the Creator and Lord.

María Clara Bingemer
Río de Janeiro, May 2004

INTRODUCTION TO THE SPANISH EDITION

This little book offers some psalms, born in the midst of our contemporary culture, which it is hoped can help accompany the process of experiencing the Spiritual Exercises of St Ignatius. There is no other intention besides being helpful. For this reason, they are to be used to the extent that they help a person to make the Exercises and should be put to one side if they distract or impede the true experience that God communicates to each person, and which is what counts. Sometimes we cannot find words to describe our own experiences, and listening to others can help us to know them better and to express them more clearly.

Some of these psalms have not been published before. Others are taken from earlier books published by Sal Terrae (in Spain) and Amigo del Hogar (in the Dominican Republic). The psalms that have come from earlier books have taken on a new aspect by virtue of being situated at various moments in the itinerary of the Exercises.

The books from which they have been taken are: *La transparencia del barro* (Sal Terrae and Amigo del Hogar, 1989), *Salmos en las orillas de la cultura y del misterio* (Amigo del Hogar, 1993), *En el aliento de Dios* (Sal Terrae and Amigo del Hogar, 1995), *La utopía ya está en lo germinal* (Sal Terrae and Amigo del Hogar, 2001) and *Orar en un mondo roto* (Sal Terrae and Amigo del Hogar, 2002).

All of us need our catechesis, our theology and our study of God to become a truly *spiritual experience*, so that our lives can be actually rooted in the living mystery of the Spirit of God in us, which every day makes all things new. Knowing things about God and belonging to a Church do not necessarily involve our affective depths, which are made in their essence for an encounter without boundaries, person to person, with the inexhaustible God.

When someone seeks out this meeting with God, a meeting which involves the whole person, *we do not know what will happen*. God is not open to manipulation, and the novelty that he offers us might not fit our accustomed words or the organizations in which we move. This is why these psalms seek no more than to *facilitate an encounter with unpredictable consequences*.

I am most grateful to the distinguished Brazilian theologian María Clara Bingemer for her help in bringing this book into existence. Her knowledge of the text of the *Spiritual Exercises*, her spiritual experience and her fine sensitivity have allowed me to select psalms that are appropriate and to link them to the text of Ignatius, from which they often arose without my knowing it. I am also grateful to her indescribable enthusiasm in translating this book for the Portuguese edition.

Benjamín González Buelta

TRANSLATOR'S NOTE

When I arrived in Cuba in the autumn of 2004, it was to learn Spanish so that I might complete my Jesuit training in Chile the following spring. The last thing I expected—or was qualified for—was to find myself working on the translation of a Spanish poet. Yet, within only a few days of my arrival, I was doing just that. The reason for the decision was simple: I found Benjamín González's poems a moving and accurate evocation of the kind of experience that I discovered taking place in my own life as I tried to live out the spirituality of Ignatius' Spiritual Exercises. He accomplishes something rare in these psalms, drawing together polarities of contemporary spirituality that are notoriously hard to integrate: justice and interiority, healing and service, the goodness of transformed humanity and the ugliness of sin. My hope is that, just as he seems to put his poetic finger on experiences which I have usually found almost impossible to articulate, the reader too will be helped by his images and language which lead us, I believe, towards an authentically Ignatian experience of God.

The original Spanish text is uncluttered and lucid; I hope I have not translated fussily. But, to some tastes, I may have done, as I have occasionally sought to avoid the baldness of a literal English rendering. It would be rash for me to offer these poems as faithful renditions of the original, but I want to thank two generous Cuban friends, Maria-Eugenia Fernández and Fr Alberto García SJ, for their help in moving my text in that direction, along with Fr Joseph Munitiz SJ, a bilingual British Jesuit, for his painstaking help in revising my draft. Of course, any infelicities that remain are my own fault.

Note that where a quotation is attributed only by a number in parenthesis, then this is the paragraph number from the *Spiritual Exercises* and is taken from *The Spiritual Exercises of Saint Ignatius*, translated by George Ganss (St Louis: Institute of Jesuit Sources, 1992).

Damian A. Howard SJ
London, January 2012

Thy world is weaving words in my mind
and thy joy is adding music to them.
Thou givest thyself to me in love
and then feelest thine own entire sweetness in me.

Gitanjali, Rabindranath Tagore

BEGINNING THE
SPIRITUAL EXERCISES

'For what fills and satisfies the soul consists, not in knowing much, but in our understanding the realities profoundly and in savoring them interiorly.' (2)

When we find ourselves seeking God, it is because God sought us first. The sense of His absence, our need to meet Him and our desire for spiritual exercises all show us that something fundamental is missing. This is one of the many ways in which *God seeks us*. God's Spirit opens our lives up to the Absolute from within the very heart of our limited personhood. 'God is missing.'

As we make the Spiritual Exercises, we are responding to God's call. We move towards a meeting of such magnitude that our whole life will find itself involved, touched and transformed. We enter into His intimacy in a communion which has no end. All we can do is 'dispose' ourselves to listen to and receive as best we can what God has to tell us of Himself and ourselves, so that we can work with Him in building a world of justice and freedom.

Two dimensions are fundamental: our disposition and God's initiative, the latter of which is unpredictable. We cannot reduce His grace to the limited understanding of things that is expressed in our humble petitions. Nor can we reduce God's new intentions to our means and calculated plans. We open ourselves to encounter an infinite goodness which always transcends our preconceptions and possibilities.

These psalms of *beginning* can help to situate us in this fundamental perspective of listening and receiving that which goes beyond our projections. So let us seek out 'him who by the power at work within us is able to accomplish abundantly far more than we can ask or imagine' (Ephesians 3:20).

Nothing to Ask of You

'The persons who make the Exercises will benefit greatly by entering upon them with great spirit and generosity towards their Creator and Lord, and by offering all their desires and freedom to him so that His Divine Majesty can make use of their persons and of all they possess in whatsoever way is in accord with his most holy will.' (5)

Today I have nothing
to ask of you;
I bear you
no complaint.
A meeting
is all I yearn for
with the infinity
that pulses inside.

How sad for me
were your answer
shackled
by my
oh so cautious question,
or by such a wounded
lament!

How sad for me
if I already knew
your answer!

In my thirst
perhaps
I would just
find
my own water
recycled,
the echo
of my drab
soliloquy,
my past
moistened
with sweat
or with tears.

3

I need you
more
than I know,
more than I can say
of myself.

Today,
here, already
in this love
with which you draw me,
I discover
the passion
that pursues me!

What Matters Most

'For what fills and satisfies the soul consists, not in knowing much, but in our understanding the realities profoundly and in savoring them interiorly.' (2)

What matters most is

> not that I seek you,
> but that you seek me in all my journeying; (Genesis 3:9)

> not that I call you by your name,
> but that you have mine tattooed
> in the palm of your hand; (Isaiah 49:16)

> not that I cry out when I am lost for words,
> but that you groan within me with your cry; (Romans 8:26)

> not that I have plans for you,
> but that you beckon me to walk with you
> towards the future; (Mark 1:17)

> not that I fathom you,
> but that you grasp me in my deepest secret; (1 Corinthians 13:12)

> not that I speak of you with great wisdom,
> but that you live in me and express yourself in your own
> way; (2 Corinthians 4:10)

> not that I keep you tight under lock and key,
> but that I am a sponge
> on your ocean-bed; (335)

> not that I love you
> with all my heart and all my strength,
> but that you love me
> with all your heart and all your strength. (John 13:1)

For how could I seek you, call you, love you …
if you do not seek me, call me and love me first?

Thankful silence is my final word,
the best way I know of finding you.

Silence

'... the more we keep ourselves alone and secluded, the more fit do we make ourselves to approach and attain to our Creator and Lord; and the more we unite ourselves to him in this way, the more do we dispose ourselves to receive graces and gifts from his divine and supreme goodness.' (20)

In the first phase,
silence is pure *privation*,
a lack, an annoying emptiness,
a being-torn-away from people and activities
that used to satisfy.
Silence feels
useless, boring,
a waste of time.
Full of the confusing reverberations
of things left behind,
it craves company,
something else to do.

If this stage passes,
silence becomes *speech*.
Hidden ghosts
come out into the light,
shrieking their demands.
Once they worked behind the scenes,
masked in activities,
plans and people,
passing almost unnoticed.
But chastened life, too,
begins to well up more vigorously,
more deeply, and we are amazed
by the depth we never knew,
which rises up inside
from our openness to the infinite.

Silence turns to *struggle*,
hand-to-hand combat,
between the phantoms, with their dragoon of fears,
and the new demands of unwearying freedom.
Silence is tense,
implacable, decisive.

In the fight, something of me dies,
something goes back to ground,
something new stakes its claim,
still marked by traces of anguish.

The face of silence has settled
into an expression of wise repose,
formed by infinite certainties
of new-born life.
Silence has made itself known as a *presence*,
serene being-in-companionship,
which opens to me the space
of its discreet love
where my harmony becomes consistent.
Silence becomes full silence,
trusting, joyful, peaceful, and now lived for the first time.
Silence is a grateful word.

The Ocean and the Sponge

'The one giving the exercises should insist strongly with the person making them that he or she should remain for a full hour in each of the five Exercises or contemplations which will be made each day; and further, that the recipient should make sure always to have the satisfaction of knowing that a full hour was spent on the exercise—indeed, more rather than less.' (12)

Down, down into your sea I sink
like a sponge,
its skin chapped
by the ravages of the sun and the road.

Seeping out of my pores
go troubled bubbles bolting,
charming their brilliance and murmur,
hollow their bursting at the surface,
pure scintillated display.

And, freer of such useless shining,
my hidden corners purified,
I soak up truth after truth.
Your water seeks and revives me.

With the voice of a drowned horizon
the deepest depth of the ocean calls me.
As my days fall towards the sea-bed
far from the compulsive swelling of waves,
a descent of darkness and silence,
my growing solitude is drenched.
And more grateful is the peace, your gift.

Thought snuffs itself out,
falling silent, speech impossible.
Neither slave nor thief,
no nerves tense as bars,
nor fright, the child of fear,
nor haste with the blood of avarice;
all my dreams and suspicions gathered together;
I just keep losing myself
in this dark, tranquil certainty.

I do not know how my speech is nurtured
in this abyss of silence.

I do not know how such life gushes forth
from this death where everything is put on hold.
I do not know how my 'I' emerges stronger
from this abandonment in which I lose myself.
I do not know how I feel you closer
the deeper I sink into your mystery.
Can any other not-knowing be so radiant?

It Is He, It Is the Silence

'… by being secluded in this way and not having our mind divided among many matters, but by concentrating instead all our attention on one alone, namely, the service of our Creator and our own spiritual progress, we enjoy a freer use of our natural faculties for seeking diligently what we so ardently desire.' (20)

Today, all creatures
refuse to let me speak.
They will not waylay
with fleeting sensations
my unending journey into the Absolute.

I close my eyes
and descend without effort,
so serenely certain
in this fond silence.
I touch the thick darkness
protecting me.
There are no bridges or profiles,
there are no steps or ambitions,
there is no yours or mine.
I hear neither harangues
nor whispers.
It is the silence, at last,
limitless,
unhesitantly receptive.
It is the great ear
who listens
to the most trivial of fantasies.
It is the mute silence
who does not contrive to convince.
It is pure existence before it blends
in sizes and colours,
before it bursts
into passions and palm trees.
It is the silence
of a mother's womb
which holds me
long enough
to be reborn for the future,
into a throng of sisters and brothers,

into the truth of everyone,
into the first ever embrace
and into laughter without cause.
It is He! It is the Silence!

Universal Mystery

'It is helpful for a person receiving the Exercises of the First Week to know nothing about what is to be done in the Second ....' (11)

The enquiry of the atheist,
the believer's prayer,
a growing love,
a tale grown weary,
one day come up
against silence,
as the only answer
to the mystery.

When we, the impatient ones,
cannot bear
the silence of the mystery,
we turn the cross into a sword,
the crescent moon into a cutlass;
we compare the waters of the Jordan
and the Ganges
as ritual ablutions,
and we cling to the catechism
like a pass to an exclusive club.
When we cannot bear
the silence of the mystery,
we deny ourselves birthings
in night-time,
or in difference,
aborting
questions and prayers,
fondness and fables.

Still, all human enquiry,
every true unease,
of whatever hue,
is a scattering of seed
in the silence
like the sowing of rice
between earth and water.
From out of the mystery,
at the ordained moment, will sprout

nourishment for all,
and it will not trouble to ask
which creed sowed it
or who its owner really is.

It has so many defenders,
and so many credit cards,
this knowledge of the mystery,
that all we have left
is the 'not knowing' of silence
before God and between ourselves:
the best soil there is
for sowing together
the seeds of a more humane future.

If we cannot
affirm the mystery together,
then together we can implore it,
and, together, await
its reply.

Total Silence

'The persons who make the Exercises will benefit greatly by entering upon them with great spirit and generosity towards their Creator and Lord, and by offering all their desires and freedom to him so that His Divine Majesty can make use of their persons and of all they possess in whatsoever way is in accord with his most holy will.' (5)

Is it possible
to speak
the silence
without breaking it?

Today the silence
is orange
and evening
like the sea.
The wounds of my body
smart
faintly,
and my fatigue
has no fibre,
no terrors.
My prayer,
unfevered,
is not a stretching of words
to enswathe
the entirety of life.

Can this calmness be
a letting go
of all I have suffered,
an opening up
to the water of life
seeping in through my pores,
confidence
without stridency,
desires
engulfed in your embrace,
anxiety
about my future surrendered
to your rhythms and surprises?

Candle Ablaze

'The one giving the exercises should insist strongly with the person making them that he or she should remain for a full hour in each of the five Exercises or contemplations which will be made each day; and further, that the recipient should make sure always to have the satisfaction of knowing that a full hour was spent on the exercise—indeed, more rather than less.' (12)

The body
before you
is a candle,
quiet
in the night
of history,
of ideas,
of plans,
consuming
the hours
like wax.

Thought
stands still
like the pointed
flame,
without the slightest
breeze
to change
its shape,
luminous
and quiet.

The heart,
crystal orange,
lit
with the peaceful
brightness
of so many infinite
encounters.

The pupils,
round
like the mouth
of an empty amphora,

dilate
in the dark,
making out
your presence.

All I hear is
the crackling
of fire,
and the breath of life
that comes
from you,
gently
rubbing
the air in which it moves.

And on seeing you
and welcoming you,
the flame lights up,
illuminating
the night,
haloing the wax,
transfiguring in light
the absences
and gloom.

And the whole person
keeps becoming
light received,
freely glowing
in your temple,
dark world
of injustices,
of fleeting stars
which dazzle
for an instant,
of restless neon
cunningly
deployed.

In the adoration
of a candle, alert
to shed light,
you make us light

from within,
no need
to carry in our hands
some ember,
borrowed and small.

Unification

Unify in yourself
my waywardness.
Switch off the seductions
hustling me towards the void.
Dissolve the fears
which petrify me in death.
Fix my desire
solely on you.
Welcome into your restfulness
what I am and what I have been.

Darkness Shining

'... so is the name of spiritual exercises given to any means of preparing and disposing our soul to rid itself of all disordered affections and then, after their removal, of seeking and finding God's will in the ordering of our life for the salvation of our soul.' (1)

You are beyond understanding.
But the darkness
of your mystery
is brighter
than our ideologies,
little lights dangling
at the crossroads.

You are beyond reach.
But your distance
is more embracing
of every last part of my being
than all the arms
which close around my shoulders
in love.

You are beyond words.
But your name,
prayed humbly,
silently pours out
more wisdom
than all the white water of words
washing round the earth.

You are beyond manipulation.
But your design
plants a drop of eternal life
even in my veins,
so all that I create
flows out
from the heart of my reality.

The Mystery in Your Hands

'In regard to the affective acts which spring from the will we should note when we are conversing with God our Lord or his saints vocally or mentally, greater reverence is demanded of us than when we are using the intellect to understand.' (3)

In your hands, Lord,
I place my mystery:
hard, at times,
not even the slightest
crack to prise open,
impenetrable surface,
steel plate.
And sometimes diffuse,
murky and changeable,
like a cloud of smoke
where my dry days
smoulder.

In your hands, I leave
my efforts and works
buried in furrows.
I will only know the truth of them
when they split open the earth
with their green leaves
and their own name.

In your hands, Lord,
I do not know what I am placing,
but I know that it is mine,
because it fires me up
and sometimes freezes me.
And I know it is yours
because, through the cracks,
I breathe a fragrance
which stills my anxiety,
and a song with no hint of shrillness
comes to me.

Thank You for Your Silence

'... offering all their desires and freedom to him so that His Divine Majesty can make use of their persons and of all they possess in whatsoever way is in accord with his most holy will.' (5)

Thank you, Lord, for your silence.
It unfurls before us
like a warm regard,
where we can try out
our apprentice words,
heartened by your fond face
gazing on us.

In your silence we utter ourselves
in a new way, our true way,
we write ourselves on to the blank page
of your welcome.
We trace our route
on your blue leaf
of a calm sea
and bright days,
or on your scorching surface
of sand and desert,
lost in history,
no tracks ahead.

Sometimes in your silence
our question grows
like a hook
in a severed hand.
Our anguish
is sharpened steel,
hard and urgent,
trying to dig
into your speechless mystery,
to sunder it
from top to bottom,
and to find you
as the only answer.
But you will not reveal yourself to us
until the time is ripe.

Despite all your self-utterance,
you will always be silence,
infinite word,
in which you will continue
revealing yourself,
that warm respect
in which we grow
to speak ourselves, to be ourselves for the first time.

The Plea of a People

'... offering all their desires and freedom to him so that His Divine Majesty can make use of their persons and of all they possess in whatsoever way is in accord with his most holy will.' (5)

Before we pray,
placing our hearts in you
and turning to talk to you,
already you have spied us
in our brokenness.
Our prayer of supplication
is only an answer
to the word your voice has sounded
in our guts.

You listen to our lumbering complaints (Psalm 69:4)
and to the cry of our community,
an oppressed people. (Exodus 3:7)
From the age-old grievance
fired into the air,
you fashion a new song
in praise of you. (Psalm 40:40)

You listen to
the huge snores we make,
worn out by howling, (Psalm 69:4)
dry as a potsherd; (Psalm 22:16)
and to the tongue that cleaves to the palate,
the bones dislocated (Psalm 22:15)
and the heart molten like wax, (Psalm 22:10)
the hands and feet pierced through (Psalm 22:10)
and paralysis certified
by years of immobility
spent in the loneliness of a rickety old bed. (John 5:6)
You bring new life
to the whole body
without our even knowing
that it was you who met us
in that strange anonymity
which cleansed us from lameness and law. (John 5:13)

You watch us
going down to the hollow of the tomb
without consciousness or speech, (Psalm 30:4)
finished off by suffering,
by the bulls and lions of power
that rip asunder and roar. (Psalm 22:13–14)
But you draw us back,
bringing us out of the grave (Psalm 30:24)
just as death,
rope in hand,
is hauling us towards the pit.

In the midst of our distress,
when we do not know what to ask for,
your Spirit makes our pain its own,
interceding for us
with wordless groans. (Romans 8:26)

Before we call you,
you answer us.
Even as we speak,
you have already heard us. (Isaiah 65:24)

Our prayer to you
is itself a sign of your saving action
among us,
making us a collective voice.

FIRST PRINCIPLE AND FOUNDATION

'... we ought to desire and choose only that which is more conducive to the end for which we are created.' (23)

We are created by God—all the time—now. In this instant the whole of creation comes right up to us and confidently accompanies us from within so that we can exist. Every creature approaches our senses like a word of God, even if sometimes we devour them without looking to see the hand that offers them.

We are constantly being *created so that we can be creators*. In this world we collaborate with God so that creation might attain its fulfilment. God needs our laboratories and our hands. He offers us the future of creation and history, but this future must pass through us, deploy our best potential and become real, bearing the traces of ourselves and of God, inseparably united.

If we are not creative we are paralyzed, we turn in on ourselves and gradually deteriorate. Simply put, we *are* not. When God's freshness passes through us, he makes us ever new and alive.

But we are not sterilised receptacles of God's gift. We are inevitably marked by the disorder of our hearts, which negates our liberty. For this reason, we need to find God in a way which frees us from all that is twisted, separating us from Him and His plan of salvation.

The most important thing is to *awaken our desire* so that we do not stay confined to whichever more or less good occupation the world might present to us, but rather are centred solely on God and His Kingdom, so that we can do the maximum possible, given whatever the Lord's concrete novelty puts to us in every situation. His call will respect entirely who we are, just as it will raise possibilities that we had never thought about but that were latent within us; they will come to life and surprise us all.

The Only One

'Human beings are created to praise, reverence, and serve God our Lord, and by means of doing this to save their souls. The other things on the face of the earth are created for the human beings, to help them in the pursuit of the end for which they are created.' (23)

In the whole universe,
no other creature
turns its face
towards you
when you call me
by my name.

When I call you
by your name
you do not mistake my accent
for any other creature
in the whole universe.

Take No Notice, Lord

'To attain this it is necessary to make ourselves indifferent to all created things.' (23)

Do not consent to show yourself
where I seek you;
guide my searching
to the place of your choosing.

Do not hasten to answer
my trifling petitions;
startle them with a goodness
beyond measure and calculation.

Do not leave me smug
for encapsulating you in concepts;
prise them open so that I may know you
as the one who will not be contained in certainty.

Do not travel with me down roads
that lead to the destination I have set;
waylay me, divert me
down the lanes of your future.

Do not let me encase you,
possess you in my breast;
unwind me fully and joyfully
in the ceaseless play of your life.

Take no notice of me, Lord,
contemplate my whole being,
listen to my millennial roots
and to that ambiguous clarity of my desiring.

Hearken to me in the Spirit
which, abiding within me,
expresses me inside you
beyond all telling.

Discreet Creator

*'... it is necessary to make ourselves indifferent to all created things ... we ought not to
seek health rather than sickness, wealth rather than poverty, honor rather than dishonor,
a long life rather than a short one .... Rather, we ought to desire and choose only that
which is more conducive to the end for which we are created.' (23)*

No need to think of the air
for it to filter through
to the last nook of the lungs;
no need to imagine the dawn
for it to swathe a new day,
at play with colours and shadows.

No need to issue orders
to the faithful old heart
or to the numerous cells
for them to fight for life
to the very last breath.

No need to intimidate
the birds to make them sing,
to stand over cornfields
to make them grow,
to spy on rice seeds
to turn them into
the earth's own secret.

In an exact dose
of light and colour,
of song and silence,
life reaches us unawares,
a gift which is ever yours,
worker without Sabbath,
discreet God.
Lest your infinity
should startle us,
you give yourself in the very gift
that hides you.

Uniting My Desires

'... we ought to desire and choose only that which is more conducive to the end for which we are created.' (23)

Necessities and desires
exact their daily toll
inside us.
They ambush the heart,
indiscriminately
strewing their anomie.

Capricious and fleeting,
like the tantrum of a child;
staples, like the sun
and daily bread;
coming at us from the world outside
with the savvy of the marketplace;
viscerally ours
with their long-drawn-out history
of hormones and a thousand days.

Yet I find within me
a desire whose roots
go deeper than I do,
with a destiny
that reaches further
than my singular shapes,
more lasting
than days I could ever count:
the yearning for you and for your Kingdom!

The only desire
that harmonizes
the orchestra of our needs,
the inextinguishable fire
which you feed every day,
intense like a naked flame
or gentle like ashen embers.

When your desire is mine,
when my desire is yours,
when the desire is ours
and one,

then heaven and earth
have come together,
eternity without count
and time measured out,
the 'I' so alone
and the 'we',
the free spirit
and the body here and now.
We only move forward
in your grace,
only following
what you hold out to us,
free of despotic appetites
whose heavy beat possesses us,
and of the demands of other masters
which tear us apart.
Only
in you and in your Kingdom.
Only. (cf. 23)

Free Me from Myself

'… to attain this it is necessary to make ourselves indifferent to all created things, in regard to everything which is left to our free will and is not forbidden.' (23)

Here I am, Lord,
bent double
like a question
mark,
waiting for
the answer
to the urgent rhythm
of despotic desire.
Unbend my question
and make of it
a sign of grateful admiration.

Here I am, Lord,
empty
like the palm of a hand,
cupped hollow,
pleading for water,
insistent, pressing.
Ease these
anxious beggar's fingers
into an agile gesture
of dance and praise.

Here I am, Lord,
curved
like a sharpened hook,
stalking
with steely precision
the tangible prey,
just recompense
for its taut exertion.
Soften my rigidity
in the gentle swinging
of a fishing-line over the waves.

Here I am, Lord,
welcoming your gift,
the joy and peace
of your mystery.

Lord of the Right Closeness

'The other things on the face of the earth are created for the human beings, to help them in the pursuit of the end for which they are created.' (23)

Any moment is a gate
to enter at the right time.
Every inch is a land
bearing your imprint.
Each colour and each smell
let me feel your imagination
as it plays towards infinity.
Every glance takes on
the intimacy of your mystery.
Every swing of the hoe
falls upon the earth
in the certainty of harvest.
Each true song
purveys to my heart
a rumour of the fiesta
already begun, eternal,
at my journey's end.

Lord, you cannot vanish
into utter hiddenness:
I should perish in your absence.
Nor can you reveal yourself in all your grandeur:
I would stay engrossed
in the majesty of your glory.

You are the Lord of the right closeness,
of the necessary sacrament
which lets us shape ourselves as we go,
with neither so much cold and night
that our clay is left raw,
nor so much noonday and sun
that we are seared by your flame.

The Absolute and Its Reflections

'… to desire and choose only that which is more conducive to the end for which we are created.' (23)

Sometimes I seek
in mere reflections
what only the sun
can elucidate.
The heart grows weary
of prising open packages and presences,
and I wring in vain
the little lights
turned on for me each day.

Sometimes I insist that the sun
make crystal clear
what meek reflections
have already hinted at.
I wilt, in loneliness,
drained from braving the absolute,
contemptuous of the little creatures
which convey it to my eyes
in everyday lights.

And I do not even know
how I am to treat you!

Cast your light on the fickleness
of this confounded heart
which fails to tell apart
your flames of fullness
from campfires of camaraderie.

Always You

*'Human beings are created to praise, reverence, and serve God our Lord, and by
means of doing this to save their souls.' (23)*

If we plumb the depths
of human pain,
you are deeper yet,
integrating the wounds.

If we soar in ecstasy
you meet us there,
unlocking the moment
to new abundances.

If we feel like creators
in the heat of the forge,
you agitate us from the future
before we go cold.

If a situation surrounds us
like an armoured capsule,
you open to us an immensity
to create your word.

We always meet you,
higher and lower,
deeper inside, further out,
Love always greater,
Love always lesser,
you, infinite and with us.

Only You

'… to desire and choose only that which is more conducive to the end for which we are created.' (23)

Will finish in dissolution
each bodily embrace
which needs must let go
to grow at a distance.

Will finish extinguished
all urgent haste
so that life
can settle down in the calm.

Will finish in emptiness
every word squeezed out
that needs to spread
to soak up water.

Only you, Lord,
haste, embrace and word,
only you, Lord,
calm, space and water.

God and His Sacraments

'The other things on the face of the earth are created for the human beings, to help them in the pursuit of the end for which they are created.' (23)

Difficult
to live with you.
Impossible
to live without you.

Too late
to be able to leave you.
Too soon
to follow your cause
unaware of absences.

Inextricably
bound to your mystery.
Impossible to find
a seduction more free.

I cannot take in your plans
nor hang on to your presence.
But no one offers me
more closeness than you.

Only in ultimate solitude
do we meet
face to face.

But what would become of me
without those frequent sacraments,
daily wellsprings
where I drink in, sip by sip,
the gift of your future?

In Your Wisdom

'Human beings are created to praise, reverence and serve God our Lord, and by means of doing this to save their souls.' (23)

We exist in your wisdom.
Our scientists
are still exploring
the silent boundaries of the universe
with their space probes,
those titanic telescopes,
that allow the eye
to pierce the mystery.
They are still looking to decode
the microscopic battle
that ensues unseen
in the tiniest cell
of our brain.
In the classroom of the universe
we are seated,
childlike,
before a night of stars.

Your wisdom
is becoming ours.
A laser beam
restores sight
when applied
to the blind eye
with the tenderness
of your evangelical hand.
And an injection of bone-marrow
allows the lame man of Capernaum
to walk,
ridding himself
of his wheelchair
and his enforced Sabbath.

We have accepted the challenge
of your unfinished *opus*.
We can render
the wasteland an oasis,

cultivate in winter-time
the fruits of summer,
and operate in the womb
on a child condemned
to be stillborn.
The poets were the first to fly;
after them came the inventors,
higher than eagles,
faster than the clouds,
through the blue of the sky.

Only as creators
can we be creatures,
united hand in hand
with you
in the same enterprise,
without ever knowing
where your gifts stop,
and our initiatives begin.

We Exist from the Unlimited

'… we ought to use these things to the extent that they help us towards our end, and free ourselves from them to the extent that they hinder us from it.' (23)

We set limits on ourselves
and we belittle each other,
yet we live in communion
with the Unlimited.

We doubt ourselves
and devalue one another,
but we go under the gaze
of Goodness.

We divide ourselves,
we confront each other,
yet we all receive life
from the One.

We classify ourselves
as perfect or misshapen,
but are all indwelt
by Beauty.

We fear our darkness,
we hide ourselves,
yet we are enlightened
by Truth.

Who could
place limits
on God's love
for us?

Who could put
limits on us
if only we could dwell in the
love of God?

Fullness Revealed in an Instant

'... to desire and choose only that which is more conducive to the end for which we are created.' (23)

To concentrate all my span
in a fraction of a second,
gather my entire endeavour
in one hand,
utter my whole personality
in a single word
and surrender myself ....

But a whole life is needed
to welcome you, to become and give myself.
An entire history is needed
to complete my solidarity with humanity;
time without end is needed
to never finish finding you—and finding me.

From the transcendence that steeps my bones
you free me from the nostalgia
of impossible totalities,
for in each of my fragments
your presence is already revealed.

Present Everywhere

'The other things on the face of the earth are created for the human beings, to help them in the pursuit of the end for which they are created.' (23)

Where can I go from your spirit?
Or where can I flee from your presence?
If I ascend to heaven you are there;
If I make my bed in Sheol you are there.
(Psalm 139)

You herald yourself in speech:
and emerge in silence.

You show your love in the gift of life:
and accomplish your self-surrender in the gift of your death.

You are dazzling in the prodigy of the day:
you enthral us in the mystery of the night.

The holiest ones are the summit of your creation:
and the most iniquitous, the pinnacle of your fidelity.

The oppressed are the expression of your liberating power:
and of your patience and respect, those who oppress them.

You are the untiring artist in all that is beautiful:
strong, still presence in all that is malformed.

Geniuses tell of your boundless possibilities:
the broken of your probing questions, posed in solidarity.

You show your masterpiece only when all of history is run,
but even now you can illuminate the fullness of the ephemeral
      instant.

You call us without end from the horizon,
you imbue us with your presence at every twist in the path.

I will never capture you in the greed of perfection,
but your light and future already flow beyond my limits.

Footprints

'... it is necessary to make ourselves indifferent to all created things, in regard to
everything which is left to our free will and is not forbidden. Consequently, on our
own part we ought not to seek health rather than sickness, wealth rather than poverty,
honor rather than dishonor, a long life rather than a short one ....' (23)

Which footprints
will lead me towards finding you?
I do not wish to live, aimless and empty,
staying simply in your footsteps.

Will they go by the name of health
or sickness?
Will they present themselves with the face of success
or with the battered weariness of failure?
Will they be arid as the desert
or teeming with life like an oasis?
Will they glimmer with the translucence of the mystic
or will they be snuffed out in the stripping of the subjugated?
Will they come down on me in a lash of the whip
or draw near in tender caress?
Will they flow in communion with a village festival
or from my primordial, unutterable solitude?
Will they be a lustrous history written up in books
or its hidden underside of oppression?

It doesn't matter which path
leads me to find you.
I do not want to grasp at your footsteps
when they are a scintillating reflection of your glory,
nor to disown them and flee
when they strike or perturb me.

It doesn't matter how long it takes
to unfold the mystery that hides you,
and each step of yours calls out my name.
My whole journey ends here
in silence and in the expectation
of a deeper 'not knowing'.
But even as I linger outside your door
'I know' that I am within you.

43

THE FIRST WEEK

'What have I done for Christ? What am I doing for Christ? What ought I to do for Christ?' (53)

All you have to do is open your eyes to see how the moral evil we call sin has spread to the whole world. Injustice and war, personal attacks and conflicts of all types, which we drag like heavy chains around our ankles throughout history, fill every day with blood and suffering. All of us are exposed to this harmful evil, and if we look at our own biography we will discover its presence, either clearly and conclusively or subtly and disguised. The 'mystery of iniquity' (2 Thessalonians 2:7) touches us all and will always continue to threaten us.

Each of us can say, 'I am a sinner, but a forgiven sinner'. God's forgiveness, when it is embraced, can restore to life people, institutions and history. Forgiveness does not just mean that God forgets our sins, but that He transforms us so that we can be different and create the new life of God in the world. We cannot feign ignorance of our sin, because it makes war on us from our inner darkness. Nor can we remain crushed by the discovery of the evil inside us or of the evil that tries to destroy us through the social structures, institutions and people we serve. With forgiveness, the Lord offers us the joy and celebration that help us to undertake a future of creativity and life. If others, or we ourselves, look on us with contempt, keeping us locked in our past, we can look at the regard of God which settles on us with love, opening the future for us. Sin is stronger than we are, but not stronger than the goodness of God within us.

Ambiguity

'... that I may perceive the disorder in my actions, in order to detest them, amend myself, and put myself in order ... that I may have a knowledge of the world, in order to detest it and rid myself of all that is worldly and vain.' (63)

Out of mystery
gushes ambiguity,
grafting body's thickness
to spirit's subtlety.
It travels undercover
with well honed ideas,
bright feelings
and inborn hungers.
It goes round with its gospel mask,
shrewdly insinuating itself
into my sure routines,
into the haste of my needs
and into the day-dreams of my repose.

But my ambiguity
starts to surface
in the unfamiliar hand,
which eludes being met,
by a slight disorder
that glances out of eyes,
by a bitter little taste
in the middle of the applause,
by a snug uneasiness
like the dregs of daily fatigue.

If I catch it unawares in its ploy
it falls back
to my bleakest depths
where light and darkness
remain to be sifted.
Wounded by clarity,
it leaves a decoy trail,
haemorrhaging in flight.
And it burrows itself in,
inaccessible, out of the reach
of my eyes or understanding.

Lord of my depths,
abyssal and unknown!
As you did on the first day of creation,
seek me and free me;
where there is darkness and deceit,
by your Spirit bring forth order
out of my primordial chaos!

The Questions God Puts

'... that I may feel an interior knowledge of my sins and also an abhorrence of them.' (63)

'Where are you?'
asks the Creator.

'Where is your brother?'
asks the Father.

'Who freed you?'
asks the Lord.

'Where are your accusers?'
asks the Shepherd.

'Why are persecuting me?'
asks the Brother.

'Why are you afraid?'
asks the Friend.

Questions from God,
like rain
on our soil,
which falls from heaven
and rises to heaven,
questions with no endpoint,
questions eternal
in the life
that they bring us
and the death
that they discard.
Received
like rain,
they set about building us
eternity now.

Forgiveness Without Conditions

'... an exclamation of wonder and surging emotion, uttered as I reflect on all creatures and wonder how they have allowed me to live and have preserved me in life.' (60)

You festoon us with forgiveness.
You do not ask us to haggle with you
over punishments or deals.
'Your sin is forgiven.
Do not sin any more.
Go and live without fear.
And do not lug around the dead body of the past
on shoulders that are free.'

You do not ask for security
on the unpayable debt
of having turned against you.
You offer us a new life,
no need to labour,
overcome by anguish,
paying off the interest
of an infinite account.

You forgive us wholeheartedly.
You are not a God
who apportions percentages of love.
'To this one seventy-five
and to this one only twenty-three.'
We do what we do,
we are sons and daughters, one hundred per cent.

Your pardon is for everyone.
Not only do you carry the lost sheep
on your shoulder,
but the wolf too,
stained with the sheep's blood.

You always forgive.
You leap up to welcome us
on the road of return,
seventy times seven;
neither turning your face from us
nor rationing out your words,
for our repeated running away.

And with forgiveness you grant us joy.
You do not want us chewing over
our broken past
in some corner of the house
like a wounded animal,
but celebrating the feast
with all our brothers and sisters,
dressed in party-best and perfumed,
entering into your joy.

We ask you in the *Our Father*
'Forgive us as we forgive.'
Today we ask you still more:
teach us to forgive others,
and ourselves,
as you forgive us.

Made Sin

'Imagine Christ our Lord suspended on the cross before you, and converse with him in a colloquy: How is it that he, although he is the Creator, has come to make himself a human being? How is it that he has passed from eternal life to death here in time, and to die in this way for my sins?' (53)

In our flesh
you have lived through
dread,
wound,
condemnation
and burial.
And now,
from the heart
of sin,
co-mingled with it
and accursed,
you stagger us,
rising out of the blue
through the self-same core
from fear,
from the lash,
from the siege,
from the pit,
and amidst
the spectral terror
of your radiant being,
in the swell
of our broken night,
you whisper to us
with the brand new voice of a friend,
 'It is me. Do not be afraid.
Come, walk on the water.'

Here I Am, Lord

'... reflect on yourself and ask: What have I done for Christ? What am I doing for Christ? What ought I to do for Christ?' (53)

Here I am, Lord,
churned up by the plough from top to bottom,
despoiled of the old harvest,
not even a single green blade left to my name.

Here I am, Lord,
the iron plough
has turned me
inside out,
frail gut
and hard rock
in the open air.

Here I am, Lord,
at the mercy of scorching sun
and the night's dew,
just an open furrow,
wounded by hope,
ready for the new seed.

Here I am, Lord.

Looking Ahead

'I will conclude with a colloquy of mercy—conversing with God our Lord and thanking him for granting me life until now, and proposing, with his grace, amendments for the future.' (61)

I look
back
and see
my sufferings
of late,
unburied,
and all of my life,
ambiguous,
generous too,
already underground,
interred
under shovelfuls
of days
and oblivions.

I look
forward
and see myself
in the life
I engendered yesterday
as I sowed myself,
and which is growing today
in front
of me
in the guileless laughter
of children,
in the rhythm
of young people
opening up
new horizons,
in communities
united
against the forces
of death.
In all of these,
this life of mine

goes before me,
mightier than me,
marking out
my path,
setting my steps.

This day,
in this very instant,
I choose
the future
and rise.

Seeming Contentment

'I will call to memory all the sins of my life, looking at them year by year or period by period. For this three things will be helpful: first, the locality or the house where I lived; second, the associations which I had with others; third, the occupation I was pursuing.' (56)

'Woe to you who are laughing now, for you will mourn and weep.' (Luke 6:25)

Woe to those

who savour the sweetness of sugar on fine china plates
but have not the palate for the bitterness of the Haitian
who cut the cane;

who gaze upon the splendid façades of imposing buildings
but cannot hear the very stones yell out with the cries of
underpaid workers;

who cruise down brand new boulevards in luxury cars
but have no memory for the families carted off like trash;

who flaunt elegant garments on pampered bodies
but scorn the hands that gathered the cotton;

for their tourist's glance glides over life,
and they do not gaze on what lies hidden behind the
facade with prophetic eyes!

Woe to those

who see in the poor man merely a hand that begs
and not an imperishable dignity seeking justice;

for whom a crowd of marginalised children is a pestilence
and not a hope for all, in need of cultivation;

who hear in the cries of the poor only chaos and danger
and not God's protest against the strong;

who only contemplate the fit, the fine and the mighty,
not looking for deliverance from the lowest and the least;

for they will never contemplate the salvation
bursting forth in a marginal Messiah.

Thank You That I Am Just like Everyone Else

'... what am I ... what is all of creation when compared with God? and then, I alone— what can I be?' (58)

I give you thanks, Lord,
for making me just like everyone else.

I strive to be secure in myself,
faced with your absence:
I balance the books
so I shall not be surprised
at the close of the day's trading.

I measure myself against others
and peer down my nose
at those who judge sinners;
and it is in comparison, not in you,
that I have put my trust.

I have also invented
fashionable denunciations
we publish at the service
of the empire-makers;
but I veil in ambiguity
my age-old sins,
radical traps for you,
an abysmal chasms for the other.

I also have my securities,
savings and tithes,
little stashes of cash
I use to haggle with
when I will not surrender to your mystery.

I also end up satisfied
listening to myself
as I stand there in the middle of the temple.
And, just like everyone else,
I can still unlock your forgiveness,
beating my breast,
beside the publican. (Luke 18:4–14)

The Poor, Sign of Contradiction

'... to ponder these sins, looking at the foulness and evil which every mortal sin would contain in itself, even if it were not forbidden.' (57)

'This child is destined ... to be a sign that will be opposed so that the inner thoughts of many will be revealed ....' (Luke 2:34–35)

The people we invite into our stores
we turn away from our tables.

We fence them in with wire in our factories,
we chase them with dogs from our houses.

We seduce them with billboard grins,
we cut them off when they come close.

We welcome them if they bring money and work,
we shun them when they seek justice and encounter.

We crush in minutes a living slum,
we pore over the positioning of a lifeless statue.

We gather them in with pledges at election time,
we scatter them with bullets when they demand their rights.

We sign them up when they are youthful strength,
we sweep them out when they are pressed rinds.

We admire them when they put up our mansions,
we shut them out with the very walls they built.

We give them charity when they are young and weak,
prison and mistrust when they are worthy and strong.

We acclaim their beatitude in books and sermons,
when they are close they do not impinge on the meaning of our
    lives.

We greet you, Jesus, when you are goodness and forgiveness,
we keep you out when you are admonition and justice.

Like all the poor of our streets,
you are a sign of contradiction.

The Cry of All History

'Imagine Christ our Lord suspended on the cross before you, and converse with him in a colloquy: How is it that he, although he is the Creator, has come to make himself a human being? How is it that he has passed from eternal life to death here in time, and to die in this way for my sins.' (53)

'Then Jesus cried again with a loud voice and breathed his last.' (Matthew 27:50)

All the cries of humanity
fit into your one cry from the cross,
from the child's first cry
to the last sigh of the death-bound.
When words are small and unable
to put across the fullness of our pain
then body and spirit rally
in this disjointed spasm.

Yours is the call of the advocate
of the new justice,
crying out to heaven for all ages,
for suffering locked up
in chambers of secret torture,
for the tears of just hearts with no escape,
stifled in private,
for all the ill-treatment of powerless minorities
and the exploitation of those muzzled
by rulings, rifles, managers and machines.

In your cry we hear the protest of God
against the rape of his children.
In you cries the Spirit, crucified
by courts, prelates and potentates down the ages,
seeking to silence a future that is free and just.
Latin America's young rebels
and the black majority of South Africa
cleave to your crucified reproof.

In your cry, fired into the heavens,
all who feel forsaken,
in unfathomable mystery,
commend their lives to the Father's hands.
From the disconcerted complaint

of those who, on occasion, sense your love
but who now feel abandoned,
and whose only hope for escape lies in the struggle with you,
from all the nights of the spirit,
our cry reaches your Father's hands.

In this, your last cry,
human pain and pain of God,
we bow our weary heads
and give up our spirit to you
as we reach our limits
where effort and days are snuffed out
and we begin to rise with you.

You Recreate Us

'I will conclude with a colloquy of mercy—conversing with God our Lord and thanking him for granting me life until now, and proposing, with his grace, amendment for the future.' (61)

In the tree of life
shine thousands of offerings
like the shining of paradise
within arm's reach.
Our fruits
are so slow to ripen!
And the creator does not arrive
till late afternoon
to see us at sundown! (Genesis 3:8)

'In God's absence
let us play at being like gods.
Let's quicken the pace of the blood,
subjugate the workers,
kick out the weak,
procure some smart weaponry,
slash through the laws of conscience
with drugs,
rip off the clothes
that shelter our identity.
Let anxiety and instinct
dance in the shadows
around idols of gold.
Let's blaze like fireworks
in the firmament of a night,
burning up the legacy of ages.'

At dawn, what has become of us?
Like pieces of a spent rocket,
we haul ourselves out, deep in sludge,
trampling one another underfoot.
The workers we paid so poorly
cry out in the stones of the buildings
in defiance of the paintwork and the mirrors.
While we were sleeping off our over-indulgence,
the forces of death

have occupied our streets.
We are branches cut off from the trunk,
falling to the ground,
intimacy used and disposable.
Our loneliness appears
as infinite abyss.

But you come up to us,
tirelessly seeking us out
in back-alleys and boulevards,
in waylaid solitude
and august gatherings.
You anoint our eyes with lotion,
cleansing us tenderly
of the wraithlike image
of the night of our seduction.
You rescue us from the mire with your hand,
clipping our damaged leaves,
bathing us with baptismal waters
and grafting us on to the tree of your life.
You hug me, arms right round,
in unconditional forgiveness.
Like a grain of frankincense,
nostalgia for the paternal home
sets the soul dreaming again.

The world is ours once more.
Only now we can be like you,
coming close to every person,
with unconditional forgiveness,
discovering your gifts each day
and building paradise with you.

Sinner's Joy

'I will consider who God is against whom I have sinned, by going through his attributes and comparing them with their opposites in myself ....' (59)

You were told:

> keep your name unblemished
> like a good Pharisee.
> You fast and save
> on the right days,
> and your life's paperwork
> is all signed and dealt with.
> Do not worry about reaching out
> to the AIDS-sufferer,
> saluting his past
> or asking his name
> as you look him in the eye.
> The poor are a bottomless pit
> of ignorance and sloth,
> devouring everyone around them
> along with their time and their goods.
> The anxiety of the loner
> can suck in your friendship
> like the vortex of a sinking ship.
> Perhaps a charitable donation will be enough,
> phoned in
> to the cold hand
> of a bank account.

But the Word says:

> the sinners and the excluded
> call out to God,
> and God comes down to them.
> We find them together
> in the same gathering:
> prostitutes from the street,
> illegal immigrants,
> prisoners under lock and key.
> God mired in the failure
> of sinners and the forlorn,

the Holy Name
crushed by machinery
of industrial steel
and by personal shame.
Here we discover
the imperishable dignity
of those who are called
the scum of the earth.
A God of such solidarity
steals our hearts
and regales us with the joy
of giving up our lives
for the universal feast
which makes everything new.

Liberating Limit

'I will conclude with a colloquy of mercy—conversing with God our Lord ....' (61)

My limitation, once accepted,
frees me
from the impossible task
of attaining the perfection
of inches and directives.

My ambiguity,
which pervades everything,
frees me
from naïveté
in relationships and plans.

My sin, forgiven,
frees me
from the pride that raises
my heart and eyes
over the heads of those around me.

My fragility, admitted,
frees me
from building my life
on self-sufficiency,
crushing and vain.

My failure
frees me
from the fear of defeat
which suffocates my imagination
and freezes the future.

My past death
frees me
from spectral dreads,
their chiefs and condemnations,
their pits and demons.

Today my knowledge
is like a child's clothes
hanging in the wardrobe,

coloured garments
that fitted me
for a stretch of the journey.
Pitiful skills
decorated with titles and seals,
archived under key,
catalogued in my bookcase
like a paper army.

But today the mystery
opens out inescapably into
an abyss at the end of all my knowing,
with its weapons of reasons and maps.
And today my ignorance
is a balm which bathes my eyes,
a fast which relieves my reasoning,
an undefended respite
without technique or timetable,
a hidden door
open to the future,
uselessly patrolled
by the mighty and the wise.

And an unimagined sustenance
issues from the mystery,
unannounced, unlabelled,
a whiff of New Year's Day,
a hope which disarms
my buttressed rationalisations.

Opening his arms to me in the night,
the only certainty
which does not devour my past,
the mystery is a Thou
who does not mock what little learning I have,
the trusty friend who, like a guide dog,
brought me to Him.

THE SECOND WEEK

'... *interior knowledge of Our Lord, who became human for me, that I might love him more intensely and follow him more closely.*' (*104*)

Not only are we pardoned sinners. We are also sinners *who have been called*. Our inimitable originality has to be expressed in the world; we have a special contribution to make within God's plan across the centuries.

If God has something to ask of us then He also has a way of making it known to us. For this we need to contemplate and discern. So, we contemplate the person of Jesus, putting him at the centre of our attention. Again and again we will interpret the unfathomable mysteries of his life, hoping that what is hidden inside them will be revealed for each one of us in this specific moment of our own lives, in this concrete reality of ours which God loves, respects and seeks to free.

We endeavour to see clearly what He is asking. But we are not naïve. We know that we live in a world that bombards the gates of our senses with stimuli so that they are driven deep into our inner recesses to appropriate our thoughts and decisions. We are overtly tempted to reject the path of Jesus. We are also tempted 'under the appearance of good', so that we might fall into the trap and believe that we are serving God while our actions deny and oppose Him.

This is why discernment is needed, examining the thoughts and feelings that move within us, listening to the tensions and the peace that pass through our bodies so that we can see clearly what comes from God and gives life, and what comes from the evil one and leads to disintegration and death.

The important thing is to contemplate Jesus, to know and love him more to the point where we orientate our whole lives towards following him, because we need to make his love visible for every person in our own bodies, handed over for everyone, so as to build his Kingdom of life which excludes no one.

Looking at Me from Where You Are

'... to gaze upon Christ our Lord, the eternal King, and all the world assembled before him. He calls to them all, ... to each person in particular.' (95)

Look at me,
Jesus of Nazareth.

> Let me feel
> your free regard
> alight upon me,
> free of the slavery
> of any synagogue,
> of demands
> which do not know me,
> of the distance
> that freezes,
> and the greed
> that would buy me.

If only your gaze
could get inside
my senses,
filter through
into the
inaccessible corners
where my unfamiliar 'me'
is waiting for you,
the 'me' sown by you
since my beginning,
and propagate my future,
the green of its leaves
silently parting
this mashed earth
which entombs
and feeds me.

Let me be
within you,
to look at me
from where you are,
and feel
all those looks,

69

of mine and others',
which deform me
and cut me through,
feel them just melt away.

Corporeal Conviction

'... ask grace from our Lord that I may not be deaf to his call, but ready and diligent to accomplish his most holy will.' (91)

First was the sensation
in my weary skin.
A breeze was coming inland
off the sapphire sea,
bearing cool relief
and a taste of iodine and salt.

My emotions
began to well up,
an air
of boundless gift,
of dwelling
in the very heart
of the loving-kindness of God.

My mind said:
'God is creating me now,
today God is my creator.'
And my thoughts
followed in the footsteps
of its unfettered imagination,
creating forth in a mystery
which defies my understanding.

From the heart
of my freedom, I said,
'Here I am.'
A turn of phrase denoting something received,
a resolution to surrender,
to be a maker of life
out of life received from God.

The conscious sensation,
the intimation of gratuity,
the incandescent thought
and the decision conceded
were taking flesh,
corporeal conviction,

transfigured body,
in the judicious repose
of stilled contemplation.

And setting out on the road,
this body of mine began to utter
its conviction within history,
in devoting all its strength
to the enterprise of the Kingdom,
and in mingling simply,
freely among the people,
bereft of lofty notions or plans.

An Intimacy Full of People

'... to gaze upon Christ our Lord, the eternal King, and all the world assembled before him. He calls to them all, ... to each person in particular.' (95)

The mystery
calls me
by my name.
And I let myself
be called
and carried.

Pierced
by people,
woven
with their cries
and chains,
their tenderness,
their rebelliousness,
I move forward
in the hollow
of your arm.
In the deepest place
I am not alone.
I find I am
full of names,
badly written
in the margins
of city
pages,
where the legitimate
letters
end,
in polluted
marshland,
cracking
against crags,
under the threat
of an avalanche,
in rivers
of scant flow,
eking out

an existence
between the greedy
fences
of landowners
and the current
of water
which dribbles along,
surveying
its occupied
banks,
awaiting
the reinforcement
of torrential
rains
to flatten
everything
and recover
its geography.

In the midst
of the encounter
I find that I am
peopled
by presences.
Children
from the neighbourhood,
barefoot,
and with a joyful
rhythm
of hungers
and smiles.

Men
bent double,
with fatigue
nailed to their backs.
Women
with
spasms of motherhood,
big-hearted
labours
and abrupt
deaths.

In the depths of
the mystery
I discover them,
you embrace us
and I meet myself.

Contemplation

'... see the various persons .... listen ... to what [they] are saying .... consider what [they] are doing .... Then I will reflect on these matters, to draw some profit from each of them.' (106–108)

When will I become pure silence
in the abyss of your deep sea,
like a sponge
with myriad pores?

When will I become trusty tranquillity,
like the palm tree on the plain
waiting for the sun to rise,
to light it up?

When will I become total attentiveness,
like the virginal eyes
of all earth's childhood
receiving without snare or suspicion?

When will I become supple freedom,
like the breeze in which you pass,
bearing the seed and the caress
and the discreet puff of life?

When will I become entire death,
like fire gifted in the night,
with all my truth risen
amidst a village festival?

The Logic of God

'... behold and consider what they are doing; for example, journeying and toiling, in order that the Lord may be born in greatest poverty; and that after so many hardships of hunger, thirst, heat, cold, injuries, and insults, he may die on the cross! And all this for me! Then I will reflect and draw some spiritual profit.' (116)

Where the city ends
and fear begins,

where the roads fizzle out
and the questions start,

near to the shepherds
and far from the landlords,

in the warmth of Mary
and winter's chill,

hailing from eternity
gestating in time,

mighty salvation for all,
in new-born frailty,

liberator from all yokes,
bound by imperial decree,

brought down to an animal's manger,
the one who will raise us all to the heavens,

is born the Son of the Father,
Jesus, the son of Mary.

Only down here is to be found the Lord of the world
whom we imagine to dwell in the heights.

God's greatness is found here,
contemplating the meekness of this little thing.

Here is the logic of God,
shattering the talk of the wise.

Here already is God's entire salvation
which will fill all nations and ages.

Jesus

'I will beg favors according to what I perceive in my heart, that I may better follow and imitate Our Lord, who in this way has recently become a human being.' (109)

Jesus of Nazareth,
word without end,
in your little name,
infinite caress,
in your worker's hands,
forgiveness of the Father,
in streets without liturgy,
Almighty Lord,
in homeless sandals,
apex of history,
growing day by day,
brother with no borders,
in a reduced geography.

You are not a capital letter,
too big to fit
in the mouths of the littlest and the least,
but bread crumbled
between the fingers of the Father
for all simple folk.

You are ever
the water of life,
bottomless well,
in the frayed knapsack
of the future-seeker,
a blue lake
in the unsleeping hollow
of the pillow,
and a sea so immense
that it only fits
in a heart
with no doors or windows.

In you everything has been said,
though for now we drink in your mystery
sip by sip.

In you we all find our home,
but we only comprise your body,
name by name.

In you all is risen,
but we can only take on your future
death by death.

And today in each one of us
you keep growing
till every name,
race, clay and creed
achieve your stature.

God Cast Off

'... the three Divine persons gazed on whole surface or circuit of the world ... and ... they decide in their eternity that the Second Person should become a human being, in order to save the human race.' (102)

In your Son, Jesus,
you cast yourself off,
quit eternity
for the harshness of the elements
and, in a spoiled inheritance,
human with us and divine,
your love nested a flight
on wings of solidarity,
veering towards the heights,
ceaselessly lifting the horizon.

In your Son, Jesus,
you cast yourself off,
you took flesh to *utter* your closeness,
in the unheard-of pretension
of being all tongues and colours
in a flesh that is mortal and abridged,
of being a never-ending parable
of infinite inflexions for the ages,
turning up alive and pristine for all
at the lintel of the senses.

In your Son, Jesus,
you cast yourself off,
you *risked* your all with the lowly,
watched-over, excluded and failed,
to tender us Life
in vulnerable meetings,
and that defenceless cheek,
sometimes kissed in friendship,
ultimately crushed beyond remedy,
in ridicule and death.

In your Son, Jesus,
you cast yourself off,
not imposing yourself with theophanies,
with fires and sidereal frights,

nor with cunning seduction,
nor armed force,
for only in free finding
are dawns engendered
to rise up from the night
and break more divinely.

Creative Freedom

'... the second state, that of evangelical perfection, when he remained in the temple, separating himself from his adoptive father and human mother in order to devote himself solely to the service of his eternal Father.' (135)

When we cling
to things and to people
we become
prison warders,
who have to
stay in jail
to stop the prisoners
escaping.

When we allow
the bird to fly
and gold to circulate,
letting go of those
we love the most,
then we live free
to go wherever,
trying out the future
where the kingdom is breaking through.

I Will Wait

'While continuing our contemplations of his life, we now begin simultaneously to explore and enquire: In which state or way of life does the Divine Majesty wish us to serve him?' (135)

I will wait for the tree
to grow
and give me shade.
But I will nourish the waiting
with my dry leaves.

I will wait for the spring
to flow
and give me water.
But I will dredge the channels
of their muddy memories.

I will wait for the dawn
to break
and give me light.
But I will throw off my night
of shrouds and prostrations.

I will wait for the arrival
of I know not what,
and it will catch me unawares.
But I will empty my house
of all its clutter.

And when I manure the tree,
dredge the channels,
shake off the night
and empty the house,
the land and the lament
will open up in hope.

Who Can See!

'... ask for insight into the deceits of the evil leader, and for help to guard myself against them; and further, for insight into the genuine life which the supreme and truthful commander sets forth, and grace to imitate him.' (139)

Who can see
how wretched is:

gold
on the wrist,

make-up
in the mirror,

the signature
on the cheque,

the degree
framed on the wall ... !

Who can see
infinity in:

a worn-out
hand,

a face
behind bars,

a smile,
unpaid-for,

sharing the aroma
of coffee ... ?

Who can see,
with simple eye,
people
and things just as they are ... !

Who can see!

Birth

'I will make myself a poor, little, and unworthy slave, gazing at them, contemplating them, and serving them in their needs, just as if I were there, with all possible respect and reverence.' (114)

History's Heart has already
materialised in the margins.

He turns no one away,
has no arguments.

He offers himself to everyone,
being pure presence.

He is the complete mystery.
Let's be still.

Gift for No Reason

'Consider how Christ our Lord takes his place in that great plain near Jerusalem, in an area which is lowly, beautiful, and attractive.' (144)

Only if we perceive you
beyond reason
can we give ourselves
beyond reason.

Only by finding you
in the centre of nothing
can we give ourselves
for nothing.

Only by being unified
in your silence
can we hand ourselves over
in silence.

Only by resting
in your mystery
can we keep dying
into the mystery.

Thank You for Needing Us

'Consider how the Lord of all the world chooses so many persons, apostles, disciples, and the like. He sends them throughout the whole world, to spread his doctrine among people of every state and condition.' (145)

In your welcoming silence
you invite us to be your word
translated into a thousand tongues,
tailored to every situation.
You long to express yourself with our lips,
in a whisper to the terminally ill,
in the cry that throws off injustice,
in the syllable that coaches the illiterate child.

Respecting our history,
you invite us to be your hands,
to grow rice,
wash the family's laundry,
save lives with surgery,
draw near in the tenderness
of the fingers that mop the fevered brow,
or ignite the love that cheers the cheeks.

Seemingly immobile,
you send us out to scour the streets.
We are the feet that carry you close
to the most marginal of lives,
our steps gentle so as not to wake
children slumbering their innocence,
strong for going down the mine shaft
or urgently delivering a perfumed letter.

You ask us to be your ears
so that your listening has a face,
attentiveness and compassion;
so that the sorrow of your absence,
the confessions of the conscience-pricking past,
the doubt which cramps life
and the love which imparts its own joy
do not dissolve into thin air.

Thank you, Lord, for needing us.
How could you ever proclaim your intent
without someone listening to you in the silence?
How could you gaze with tenderness
without a heart which senses your gaze?
How could you confound corruption
without a prophet to put his life on the line?

Lord, Have Mercy on Me

'... that I may be received under his standard ... in the most perfect spiritual poverty ... to no less a degree of actual poverty ... in bearing reproaches and injuries, that through them I may imitate him more.' (147)

Lord, have mercy on me.

>Because I contemplated life
>I find myself committed to dying.

>Because I contemplated
>the face of the poor
>I find myself mistrustful
>of every eloquence,
>expedient and estate.

Lord, have mercy on me.

>Because I sought to pierce with my own eyes
>the mask that envelops all reality,
>to discover you as the ultimate truth
>which ushered everything into existence,
>now I find myself in this aloneness
>where only you can meet me.

Lord, have mercy on me.

>No one can seek you and die.
>No one can see you and live.

Saving Weakness

'... I desire and choose poverty with Christ poor rather than wealth; contempt with Christ laden with it rather than honors. Even further, I desire to be regarded as a useless fool for Christ, who before me was regarded as such, rather than as a wise or prudent person in this world.' (167)

From his wheelchair
this motionless paralytic
moves my feet
towards the life of solidarity.

Out of a blind girl's smile,
as she feels her way along the wall,
gleam all the colours
which my gloom had failed to see.

Through his silence, the mute
chastises my chatter,
my 'appropriate' responses,
making me a worthier companion.

The autistic child, imprisoned
in her silence of absences,
churns up my tenderness
as I seek a way in.

Broken, impaired people,
in whom God's weakness,
enfleshed in their wound,
saves the weak and saves the strong.

Seed of the Kingdom

'My will is to conquer the whole world and all my enemies, and thus to enter into the glory of my Father. Therefore, whoever wishes to come with me must labor with me, so that through following me in the pain he or she may follow me also in the glory.' (95)

How could the farmer
take the risk of sowing
if he could not already see a field of wheat
in his tightened fist
full of seed?

How can you look at the earth
through eyes of hope
without glimpsing the forest
in the winged seeds
of the oak
lifted on the wind?

How will a young couple ever dream
without intuiting
in the embryo
all the laughter
and playfulness
of children?

How can you hand yourself over
for the sake of the meek
if you do not see with new eyes
the utopia of the Kingdom
bursting open,
just managing to split
the shell of fear?

You—I

'... to ask for ... insight into the genuine life which the supreme and truthful commander sets forth, and grace to imitate him.' (139)

How can I tell
where I end
and you begin?

If I go down
into my sin,
I meet you there
in solidarity,
in an abyss
which makes me dizzy
just to look at.

If I rise
to the light
there you are, shining,
never-ending source
of my home truths.

If your light glitters
in the abyss
of my sin,
how can I tell
where I end
and you begin?

If I gather up all the things I've said
and examine them,
I see them bringing life
to so many souls
it makes me feel
giddy.

If I immerse myself
in a silence
without limit or schedule,
deeper in
and further down
I always find you.

If your word goes
in my word
and my silence
in your silence,
how can I tell
where I end
and you begin?

If I say 'I'
when you
are my origin,
ultimate and every day,
then I am also
saying 'you'.

If I say 'you'
when I am
a difference
inspired by you,
then I am also
saying 'I'.

If to say 'you'
I have to be me,
and can only be me
when I say 'you',
how can I tell
where I end
and you begin?

If I work
for your Kingdom,
I feel
shot through
with an infinite
energy.

If I contemplate
your endeavour,
I sense
an air
of delight.

If only
through my toil
can your enterprise
be fulfilled,
and only in you
do I meet
the meaning
that moves me,
how can I tell
where I end
and you begin?

Baptize Me, Jesus

'... *Christ our Lord, after his farewell to his Blessed Mother, came from Nazareth to the river Jordan, where St John the Baptist was.' (273)*

Baptize me, Jesus,
with the sun and the breeze
of your daily grace,
circumspect creation,
dripping down my brow.

Immerse my body
in the goodness of the people,
which runs along the channel
of the deep paths
their feet have cleared
as they labour and meet.

Clothe me in white,
rising from the waters,
holding my breath,
and clasp me to your bosom
in the shared embrace
of a thousand open arms.

Dissolve a grain of salt
on my palate
so that this new life
is kept utterly intact
with the sharp tang
of the gospel.

Anoint my brow
with your cross of affliction
and anoint my breast
with the pain of the people.
I will carry to Calvary
the cross of your mystery.

Let all the world rejoice
in the natural sound
of metal and wood,
and let the voices sing out
today, the first day
of the new creation.

The Eye of the Needle

'... in order to imitate Christ our Lord better and to be more like him here and now, I desire and choose poverty with Christ poor rather than wealth; contempt with Christ laden with it rather than honors. Even further, I desire to be regarded as a useless fool for Christ, who before me was regarded as such, rather than as a wise or prudent person in this world.' (167)

My life
was so narrowed down,
so squeezed in the grip
of other people's needs,
that it slid smoothly
through the 'narrow eye
of the needle'
to find you.

All the finery
pinned to my chest,
like a cache of sham treasure,
was stripped away,
so I nimbly crossed
the 'narrow path'
which leads
to the new future
of your Kingdom.

Being an outcast
and having my weaknesses
reach everyone's ears,
borne on an unruly wind,
I felt so disgraced
that I bowed my head
and entered as a brother
by the 'narrow gate'
of the true us.

God of the Underside

'... we now begin simultaneously to explore and enquire: In which state or way of life does the Divine Majesty wish us to serve him?' (135)

You and I:
we are both
a single leaf
of paper.
I am
the upper side
facing the sun and the air
and anyone who seeks
to read a word,
to hear and find you.
You are
the underside
supporting me,
dark,
invisible,
stuck to the wood.

Seeking you
I cannot swivel,
take leave of my being,
lean out
from the other side of myself,
or startle you
with a sudden change of tack
to catch you
in your mystery.
I can only
remain suspended
in the silence
of your grace
and feel how
exact life
flows into me,
from my depths,
where I receive myself
inexhaustibly
from you.

Presently,
as I set about my daily chores,
you take to the streets
within me,
embracing with my arms
and radiating
from my gaze.
My limitations do not
embarrass you,
nor does my vocabulary
curb you.

Of me you are making
a true servant
without perfect works.
Let's try out
your Kingdom together
in the intentions
of this eternal apprentice
in this land
of futures.

God underneath,
silent consistency,
I cannot tear myself
without wounding you,
nor be
your open page
unless you are
my secret verso.

Only I with you
and you with me,
can we be today
a word of yours,
embracing and gazing,
in human flesh
in this world.

God of Jesus

'A Colloquy should be made with Our Lady. I beg her to obtain for me the grace of her Son and Lord that I may be received under his standard ... bearing reproaches and injuries ... if only I can do this ... without displeasure to the Divine Majesty.' (147)

Jesus of Nazareth,
which God did you reveal to us?

You did not craft an ark, as Noah did,
to rescue yourself with the righteous.
You did not build a temple, as Solomon did,
a dwelling for Yahweh.
You did not lead, as Moses did,
a people to the promised land.
You did not beget, as Abraham did,
a host of descendants.

You, Jesus,
deluge-drowned,
life poured out in the streets,
ruined temple
in your unguarded body,
geography without frontiers
or owner's grip,
a universal tribe
pulsating in every vein,
which God did you reveal to us?

Jesus of Nazareth,
finite and embodied,
universal and executed,
the one future
so present,
which God did you reveal to us?

Sowing Newness

'Consider the address which Christ our Lord make to all his servants and friends whom he is sending on this expedition. He recommends that they endeavour to aid all persons, by attracting them, first, to the most perfect spiritual poverty and also, if the Divine Majesty should be served and should wish to choose them for it, even to no less a degree of actual poverty.' (146)

It is perfectly true.
Some of the seed
will drop on the path,
among thorns,
between rocks,
on rigid customs,
amid choking envies
and scourged backs.
And the word will be lost.

But the deeper truth is that
I feel compelled
to dip my hand
in the soul's own seeds
and hurl life into the air,
no matter the lie of the land,
not reckoning on the response
nor amassing a profit.

And following the path
may I hang on to that joy
of the open hand,
not with fists
clenched round old belongings
that cannot accept
the freshness you now feast us with.

Light

'The person typical of the third class desires to get rid of the attachment ... [desiring] to keep it or reject it solely according to what God our Lord will move one's will to choose, and also according to what the person himself or herself will judge to be better for the service and praise of the Divine Majesty.' (155)

You do not call us
to bring light to the darkness
with frail wicks
cosseted from the winds
by the palm of the hand,
nor to be pure mirrors
reflecting other lights,
sought-after stars
reliant on other suns
which, like masters of the night,
illuminate
with momentary reflections
mere surfaces
according to their whim.

You offer to be
the light within us, (Matthew 5:14)
ardent bodies,
glowing with a flame that cannot die
in the marrow of the bone, (Jeremiah 20:9)
burning bushes
in future-questing
wasteland solitudes, (Exodus 3:2)
ember in the inglenook
gathering companions
who share in fish and bread, (John 21:9)
prophetic lightning
which fractures the night
that is so truly the mistress of death.

You offer to be
the light of the people, (Isaiah 42:6)
pentecostal pyres,
as our days
are relentlessly burned off,

ignited by your Spirit,
to be aglow in you
who are light,
inseparably melted,
our fire with your fire.

Free Us, Lord, from Grasping

'... three steps: the first, poverty in opposition to riches ....' (146)

Free us, Lord, from grasping.

From attaching ourselves to wealth
like someone binding himself
with a safety belt
to the jet as it sets off to its destination.

From making ourselves
a centre of pilgrimage,
a place where all paths meet
for those who come and go
in search of the absolute.

From immolating our freedom
on the altar of technology
where we, with ravenous gulps,
are busy destroying
a future we have turned into an object.

From storing up knowledge
with the tacit intention
of vaunting our name
till it reaches, via satellite,
to the ends of the earth.

From pointing our fingers
at our own chests,
playing at being gods,
while the finger of John
pointed to Jesus among the people,
and Jesus pointed to God and his Kingdom.

Free us from all grasping;
that of the spirit and of technique,
that of fame and of money,
idols which puff us up,
intoxicating us with their fleeting glitter.
To slake our anxiety
and the void of transcendence,
they stipulate a daily ration
of blood, both our own and another's.

Primacy of the Last

'... the second, reproaches or contempt in opposition to honor from the world ....' (146)

You were told:

> always come top.
> Get the best grades
> in the school,
> make sure it is your chest that breaks
> the final ribbon
> in every race.
> Do not ever let anyone
> get ahead of you
> or sit above you
> at table.
> Dazzle all your friends,
> showing off the latest gadget,
> one of those pricey executive toys
> to wrong-foot your ennui.
> Let the next rung up
> be the only place to catch your breath.

But the Word says:

> feel the look of God
> as it settles on you,
> for He encourages
> infinite possibilities
> in your mystery.
> Unwind totally,
> be free from ties that bind you,
> from fear within,
> from murmurings on the street,
> from the greed of the investor,
> and the threats of your superiors.
> And do not be loath to settle down
> in a little chair
> with the lowliest of folk.
> There you will find, with the Father,
> the bliss of creating
> freedom and life for all,

without the drudgery of displaying
a certificate of excellence.
When the Kingdom is created,
the last of this world
just might be the first.

Servant of All

'... journeying and toiling, in order that the Lord may be born in greatest poverty; and that after so many hardships of hunger, thirst, heat, cold, injuries, and insults, he may die on the cross! And all this for me!' (116)

You have been told:

>
> surround yourself with winners.
> If your life is to be a success
> you must exploit everyone.
> Store up in your memory
> the name of that millionaire,
> and note down the phone number
> of that feminine face
> smiling in the crowd.
> Cover the walls of your house
> with the signatures of painters
> of fame and of fortune.
> Cram your mouth
> with the names
> that strut on
> the slippery stage of glory.
> Make yourself their neighbour or their mate,
> join their club or party.
> Such renown
> will lend you prestige!

But the Word says:

>
> seat at your table
> those who could not
> invite you to their home
> because it has been dragged off by the river,
> and lend without puckered brow
> to the person who cannot return your loan
> on pay-day
> because the extra hours
> got lost in the computer
> of the Special Economic Zone.
> They will have found in you
> God's answer
> to their daily anguish.

And you will sense intervening
something of God passing
through the core of your very self
to reach out to your brother.
And as this gesture
of free friendship
shatters the edicts and thrones
of carefully calculated
investment,
a fountainhead of eternity
will well up through your stones,
making you a servant of all,
brimming over with grace and savour.

The Way Symbols Beckon Us

'... and if his Divine Majesty should be served, ... actual poverty ....' (147)

The finest symbols,
the Kingdom, the poor,
justice, freedom …
sometimes beckon us;
but deep wounds
place deceptive mirrors
in the way,
turning us back in
on ourselves.
And, baffled, we lose ourselves
in the maze
of our own tortuous searches
to try and fill
our hollow selves
while we name absolutes.

The finest symbols,
the Kingdom, the poor,
justice, freedom …
can also set
our numb, routine
imaginations
on fire,
gird body and spirit
for the fray,
and unify us like the flames
that blaze in the risk
where shackles melt.
The allure of eternity
moves us along,
mingling the moment and the mission
with the absolute.

Poor and Free

'... the desire to be able to serve God our Lord better is what moves one to take or reject any object whatsoever.' (155)

Yesterday my photo captured the gesture of glee
only to awaken a vague, giddy vision today.
My words sparkled with diamantine precision;
today they appeared small, impossible, stifling.
My symbol, a brimming torrent of evocation,
is as mute today as some grotesque idol.
The hand grasped with warmth
slides frostily off my palm
like the dying of a frail bird.
Sunshine meetings and names,
just sink away, come dusk,
in the far-off horizon,
in the intimacy of my bottomless ocean.

To let go!
Why must I grasp at what I have found?
Everything I cling to
fills me with mortal paralysis,
losing its song and flight
in my golden cage.

A thousand facial expressions I have used
are mine no longer;
they lit other moments of intimacy, long since snuffed out,
no longer featuring in my dreams and tables.
I know my life, surrendered, has not died.
The day will come when I shall meet again
with all my life made gift
nameless company of solitudes,
unction of long-buried brows,
strength of daring far from home.

To let you go!
Your transcendence nests in my flesh
with my dry grass
and when it ripens and is 'mine'
it flies towards others

in gaze and creative word.
And in that hollow of unsatisfied fullness
which still remains in me
your presence nestles anew.

All that matters is that you come.
Every morning,
leaving known horizons behind,
the day drives sleep and night
out of my bones
and lights up dawning paths.

To let you go!
And in the end to have nothing,
to let go of so much.
But my fullness is found
in opening myself
to your coming!

THE THIRD WEEK

'Consider how his divinity hides itself …. Consider … what I ought to do and suffer for him?' (196–197)

Jesus was committed to proclaiming the Kingdom of God, but came up against the opposition of those who were wrapped up in their wealth or their own justice and holiness. The messiah had not come by the wide road that they had planned for him, but rather by narrow side streets. *From the very beginning of his life, a conflict begins which is only brought to completion in the cross.*

Everyone who gives himself or herself over to Jesus' cause will also encounter conflict with those who feel their interior peace or their interests to be threatened, and will experience opposition, social exclusion, punishment, even death like today's many martyrs. You cannot avoid confrontation. We will be signs of contradiction like Jesus.

The simple fact of being faithful to God's gift of life, or to the lives of the many people who are crushed each day, will bring with it the suffering of the cross. The challenge for us consists in living this conflict creatively, without letting ourselves disintegrate, dissipate or become paralyzed. *The cross is paschal, bearing within it the seed of resurrection.* To access and touch the dynamism of this eternal life, which runs through all crosses, and allow oneself to be permeated by it, enables us to experience resurrection already in the midst of our current experiences of death.

This is our challenge: to contemplate God wounded, hidden beneath the face of human fragility. God is not absent in the passion of his Son, but suffering in Jesus. Our God is vulnerable.

This contemplation communicates to us the wisdom of the cross, which is folly and scandal to many but contains a future of life and freedom for all. Already in contemplation we can experience the unequalled power that comes to us from the heart of Jesus put to death. What we have to contemplate is the love that hides itself in weakness and reveals itself in the total sacrifice of the cross. Only love can save us and allow us to be united to Jesus' cause in spite of all that threatens us.

The New Now

'Consider what Christ our Lord suffers in his human nature ....' (195)

In the mystery of the earth
new life is nurtured
in the grain of wheat
'without knowing how'. (Mark 4:27)

A wall in Berlin,
so pitted by bullets,
so stained by blood,
one day becomes
a child's plaything
'without knowing how'.

Everyone wants to lay their hands on
the ripened ear.
Few feel like being buried
like a grain of wheat
where the future is formed
'without knowing how'.

The throng floods into the streets
with dances and flags
when freedom breaks out.
Few shut themselves alive
in clandestine shadow,
feeling their way forward
'without knowing how.'

Everyone dreams of the Kingdom,
pledging it, painting it, chanting it.
Few foster it
with their insights and sleepless nights
without schedules and pay-deals,
fertilising its tiny germ,
its fragile genesis,
    'without knowing how'.

To Lose My Life

'Consider what Christ our Lord suffers in his human nature …. Consider how he suffers all this for my sins, and so on; and also ask: What ought I to do and suffer for him?' (*195, 197*)

To lose my life,
to give freedom to a soul,
to cultivate a friendship,
to heal a hope …
Delighting in the newness of it all
then they can disappear
down untravelled roads,
not leaving a forwarding address.

To lose my life,
pouring out my days
on brows regardless
of synagogue or party labels,
on good and bad
just like the sunshine and raindrops
which the Father bestows on all.
Not to bother adding up the figures
to see if our efforts
have trickled fruitlessly
over clogged skin
on to the dust of the path,
or if they have tumbled, fertile,
on to that secret place
where life is taking root.

To lose my life
like the man who stakes
his salary and sweat
or a fortune bequeathed.
The roulette wheel spins,
doctored by the managers
who run the casino
and who deem that our number
does not belong on this board.
They rob us of our efforts
and they leave us
clutching a ticket with no prize.

The renewed souls,
the giving over of our days,
the bold wager ...
are born of lives
so lost to themselves
that the Spirit of all
enshrouds them in its mystery
like wrapping paper,
ready to open when all are gathered in
for the great festival without sundown.

Good Friday Afternoon

'... sorrow with Christ in sorrow; a broken spirit with Christ so broken; tears; and interior suffering because of the great suffering which Christ endured for me.' (203)

Your life was facing oblivion,
yet you were reaching fullness.

You appeared nailed like a slave,
but you were achieving total freedom.

You had been reduced to silence,
yet you were the greatest word of love.

Death was flaunting his victory,
but you were routing him once and for all.

The Kingdom seemed to bleed with you,
but you were building it up in utter surrender.

The leaders thought they had deprived you of everything,
but you were handing yourself over for the life of all.

You would die as if forsaken by your Father,
but he wrapped you in his embrace, no daylight between you.

You would disappear for ever into a tomb,
but you were inaugurating a new presence to the whole world.

For the one who gives himself to your design,
is death not only apparent failure?

Are not we more radically free
when we abandon ourselves to your endeavour?

Are not we nearer fulfilment,
gradually dispossessed in your mystery?

And is not joy your last word,
amidst the crosses of the just?

Crucifixion

'Consider how he suffers all this for my sins, and so on; and also ask: What ought I to do and suffer for him?' (197)

Already the pain of this people
has pierced
my hands and feet
and driven
its barbed fixation
into my skull.
And in my side I bear
an open breach
where the cold is getting in
to my unguarded breast,
with protests
which prowl the streets,
seeking a heart
to lodge in.

Why have you forsaken me?
I cannot now
come down from a cross
made of people.
Father, accept
my spirit
into your hands
and on the third day
raise up this mystery.

Cross

'Consider how his divinity hides itself; that is, how he could destroy his enemies but does not, and how he allows his most holy humanity to suffer so cruelly.' (196)

A remunerated goal
requires a long,
hard haul.
But the arithmetic
gives us the confidence
that it's worth it.
Sometimes the cross
is just an *investment*.

For love of neighbour
we cheerfully expend
time, strength and money.
The cross is
solidarity with another:
someone I sense,
somehow, is part of me.

A sudden strike, like lightning,
can hit us in a split second
leaving our life
incurably impaired.
I forfeit my well-being,
a loved one
or my good name.
A green shoot
is torn out of me,
a living part of me.
When the injury
settles down,
the cross is called *acceptance*.

There is the free cross, too,
the one I choose
and from which I do not flinch;
only, once nailed,
I cannot bring myself down
as I please.

My endeavours are given over
to the nails,
my imagination to the thorns,
my name to the calumny of the crowds,
my lips to vinegar,
and my belongings are divided up.
Here, the cross is called *fidelity* to Love in Love,
which is song and strength
rising to new life by the wound.

Ember

'... calling often to memory the labors, fatigue, and sufferings which Christ our Lord suffered, from his birth up to whatever mystery of his Passion I am contemplating at the time.' (206)

To be an ember
in the centre of the hearth
it has to have burned
all the way
to the heart
of the wood.

Only then does an ember
become contained fire,
without black stains
of vegetal nostalgia
or yearning
for breezes and rivers.

The ember appreciates
the covering ash
which hides and protects it
and needs no sudden blazes
sputtering, 'See *me!*'

Its orange intimacy
warms without frightening
and in its sober tenderness
nothing is singed.
It lives slow and long,
not crackling grumbles
or seducing solitudes.

As the warm memory
of free encounters
which smile down through life,
it loves its ashen fringe.

To Wound the Infinite

'... What ought I to do and suffer for him?' (197)

God's life does not grow
out of human death,
but human fullness
out of the death of God.

God's strength does not show up
our weakness,
God's weakness
builds our strength.

For only idols
feast on the blood of others,
but God pours out his own
to save ours.

The cold wound of iron
which tears flesh
in the same blow pierces
the incarnate heart of God.

And where a blow wounds us
living water flows unendingly,
for Love can only abound
through the breach open to the Infinite.

Offered to the Father and to Us

'Consider what Christ our Lord suffers ....' (195)

You can
only offer
with unclenched fingers,
hand stretched out,
with bread that is free
and ours,
en route
to another person
like a flight,
so that what is offered may
be received,
not wrenched
by brute force,
nor seduced
by cunning,
nor acquired
by the power
of the one who pays.
There is no offertory
with clenched fists,
possessive hearts,
calculated investment.

It is not only
the arms of the priest
lifted high
with bread and wine.
They are everybody's arms,
the whole community's,
tendering
something anointed
by their labour
and elation,
the pure part of their utopia,
bread of everyone,
unblemished,
unpossessed,
a liberated loaf,

a horizon
suspended
in the heights of exertion,
convoking
all arms
towards the future.

Stretch out your arms,
Father,
and receive this bread,
this honed cosmos,
this hunk of history
reconciled.
Reach out your arms
for ours
cannot reach
to heaven;
vault the abyss
and come down.
Come, see our ovens
and markets,
our banks
and congresses,
and you will see
the arduous task
of making
bread of everyone.
Walk
through our
avenues and alley-ways,
suburbs and farms,
and you will feel the risk
of overcoming the abyss
to create a community
where bread
can be offered,
bread with room
for every heart.

The Fullness of the Poor

'Consider how his divinity hides itself ....' (196)

Lord of my friendships,
with their ultimate redoubt
beyond the reach of the hug
which seals distance and closeness.

Lord of gracious looks,
which alight upon me, tender and far off,
like the fresh breath
of deep, unfamiliar wells.

Lord of my inspired words
which, like rain,
gave life to locked-in seeds
and hid in the earth.

Lord of all those souls
recreated in meeting me,
now going happily their own way,
without my blood in their arteries
or my name in their papers.

Lord of my deepest secret,
solitary uniqueness,
future now engendered
in my hazy, unknown past.

Lord of my exuberance,
generous and squandered;
today my life smells
like freshly pruned vine.

Lord, I have neither
your autograph nor your ring.
I have nothing of yours
bar this questing,
this fissure, this gap.

Whenever I slumber in the shade
of so much that is
beautiful, noble and just,

I always awaken more eager for the road,
with an absence more orphaned,
a question more hollowed out,
my whole mystery roused
by the signs of your passing.

Today all I have is the hollow,
the nails of your cross
left in my hands.
And through those two wounds
is poured out over the whole earth
all the water I sought in vain to secure
and never lacked.

Wound

'... sorrow with Christ in sorrow; a broken spirit with Christ so broken; interior suffering ....' (203)

Today the pain is real
in my body and spirit.
Today my woundedness would invade me,
fill my heart with weary grief,
wrench me like a stampeding mob,
besiege my entire body.

This is what I am: a wounded man.
I accept the whole story of my struggling.
I love the people who have maimed me
and am at peace with my ambiguity,
spinning its traps
in my most secret depths.

I am loved by you, God of life.
And you want all you have sown
to live in me.

With this dawning day
I long to turn my eyes
to the rising sun,
awakening the colours
and rumour of footsteps on every path.
Let the peace of daybreak
run like living water
through the warrens of my secret.
Now, not tomorrow.
Now I let you dawn and recreate me.

The pain that remains does not matter.
My desire is to be united with you in the quest of life,
to risk my all with you in the journey's stakes,
to stay together with you in patience, submerged.

Way beyond anything that might fathom my secret,
all my mystery is nested in your hands
like a dove, at once trusting and fearful,
in the precise instant when it is released into the air
to take flight, play and live.

The day begins to stir.
The aroma of early coffee,
the crying of children,
brief and first-time farewells.
With all of creation,
they come alive to my first steps.

THE FOURTH WEEK

'... to ask for the grace to be glad and to rejoice intensely because of the great glory and joy of Christ our Lord.' (221)

The great proclamation of the Gospels is that *Jesus has risen from the dead*. The disciples had the spiritual experience of a fresh meeting with Jesus. He was the same—they recognised him. This unthinkable experience made only faltering progress within each of the disciples and in the community. But eventually they all found themselves transformed by the encounter and they became strong, joyful witnesses to this, the central event of history.

This is also the heart of *the experience we are looking for today: Jesus rising within whatever situation of death* is closing in the individual or communal lives like the tombstone of the sepulchre. God's future, which is our future made more just and more humane, will take the form of tearing down sepulchres to be creative, escaping not only from the power of the synagogue and of the armed force of the empire but also from the disillusionment that poisons and paralyzes life.

Not only are we responsible for this work of commitment to passion and death. We are also responsible for joy. But this joy can only be nourished by meeting with the Risen One who today brings life and freedom to every human situation. It is not only a matter of being witnesses to the Risen One of yesterday, but also to the One who is alive and confronts us today. To meet this Jesus we need to go into those situations where people are condemned to failure, injustice and grief.

Your Incorruptible Joy

'... to ask for the grace to be glad and to rejoice intensely because of the great glory and joy of Christ our Lord.' (221)

Grant us, Lord, *your incorruptible joy*!
Entertainment has its price and propaganda,
and its merchants are connoisseurs.
Fleeting escape is available on loan
with its exotic, futile means.
Enjoyment is drunk on credit cards,
and squeezed dry like a paper cup.
But your joy is priceless,
and we cannot contrive it.
It is a gift to be welcomed and bestowed.

Grant us, Lord, *your surprising joy*,
associated more with pardon received
than the pharisaic perfection of the laws.
Found more in persecution for the Kingdom's sake
than in the applause of the boss.
It grows when I share what is mine with others,
and dies in my amassing what belongs to my peers.
It intensifies in waiting on the servant class of history,
more than in being served as master and lord.
It burgeons going down with Jesus to the human abyss
and withers clambering over despoiled corpses.
It is renewed when it stakes all on an unknown future;
it is dissipated storing up the harvests of the past.
Your joy is humble and patient
and walks hand in hand with the poor.

Grant us, Lord, *'perfect joy'*!
The one that thrives like a fresh resurrection
amid the rubble of failed plans,
that neither the prison of social systems
nor random executive diktat
quite manage to wrench from the poor.
The deepest, most gutting disappointment
cannot screen us for ever
from its ceaseless initiative.
Your joy may be wronged and downtrodden,
but it is immortal from your Easter on.

Grant us, Lord, the *simple joy*,
the sister of the little things,
of daily discovery
and necessary routines.
Which moves freely among the great,
not in livery or with studied gestures,
but like a breeze, unfettered and selfless.
Your joy is trusting and sure,
and looks to the littlest of those beloved of your creatures
as residing in your heart and in your plan.

I Choose Life

'Consider the office of consoler which Christ our Lord carries out, and compare it with the way friends console one another.' (224)

This morning
I stand erect,
I open my face,
I breath in the dawn,
I choose life.

This morning
I accept my injuries,
I hush my limitations,
I dissolve my fears,
I choose life.

This morning
I look into the eyes,
I put my arm round a shoulder,
I give my word,
I choose life.

This morning
I make peace,
I nourish the future,
I share joy,
I choose life.

This morning
I seek you in death,
I raise you from the mire,
I bear you, so fragile,
I choose life.

This morning
I listen to you in silence,
I let you fill me,
I follow you intently,
I choose life.

Jesus Risen

'Consider how the divinity, which seemed hidden during the Passion, now appears and manifests itself so miraculously in this holy Resurrection, through its true and most holy effects.' (223)

Lord
of lived-in spaces
and the shapeless air,
of the leaf that strengthens
its adolescent green,
and of the ochre that folds itself
on its weary biography,
of the resolute word
and the trifling thought,
barely voiced,
of the light that falters
in the corner of the candle
and of sidereal blazes,
of the anonymous cell
and the chronic wound
which drains our pride,
how can you knit
fire with water,
the wounding spear which is the mouth
with the mouth-like spear-wound in the flesh,
the contracted usury
of white skin
with black skin
in creaseless dance,
the bomb that exterminates,
falling from the skies,
and orphaned innocence
shielding its head
with a pillow?

I hold my tongue.
Not that my silence is
a deserted house
or a wound with no cure.
It is earth ploughed
by the steel blade of solidarity.

My waiting grows long like a furrow,
a flat certainty in the earth
open wide
to the Heights.

Death and Resurrection

'Consider how the divinity, which seemed hidden during the Passion, now appears and manifests itself so miraculously in this holy Resurrection, through its true and most holy effects.' (223)

When my friend died
something of me
which was yet him
vanished.
Something of me
rose in him.
Something of him
which still is me
remained.
Something of him
is awaiting resurrection in me.

As time goes by
it appears to wipe out
all love.
But the more my memory
fades into the past,
the closer I get
to that encounter without distance
of the future.

Although for me
every day has
its pruning, its waiting and its harvesting,
for him
the whole of history is accomplished;
I arrived there with him
and there is where I am.

Thank you, Lord.

Such a Pauper, Such a God!

'... the grace to be glad and rejoice intensely because of the great glory and joy of Christ our Lord.' (221)

How poor is
the one who has discovered
the pain of the world
as the pain of God,
the injustice of the peoples
as rejection of God,
the exclusion of the weak
as an assault on God!

    The cross is his for certain!

How blessed is
the one
who has discovered
in the protest of the poor
the bursting of the tomb;
in the marginal community
the future of Jesus;
in the littlest ones who welcome us
the mothering lap of God.

    Her resurrection has already begun!

How poor are
they who have met
such a pauper,
such a God.

    How blessed are they!

Apparitions

'Consider how the divinity, which seemed hidden during the Passion, now appears and manifests itself so miraculously in this holy Resurrection, through its true and most holy effects.' (223)

You appeared
when the soul
was in no hurry
to arrive,
to grow
or to die.

When you left
the body
produced no balance-sheet
of absences,
of caresses
or of questions.

And you left me with
a surprise
a certainty
a heart.

You never went!

Lost Creatures

'Consider the office of consoler which Christ our Lord carries out, and compare it with the way friends console one another.' (224)

What becomes of:
the sowing with no harvest?
the pregnancy with no birth?
the torture with no freedom?
the insomnia with no answer?

Where do they go,
those creatures lost
according to our reckoning?

Nothing is lost!
Everything returns
to the mothering soil,
making lush humus
where the future grows.
They will return, one by one,
to our table
as tomorrow's flower,
more free,
and more ours.

The Meaning You Seek

'Consider how the divinity, which seemed hidden during the Passion, now appears and manifests itself so miraculously in this holy Resurrection, through its true and most holy effects.' (223)

The meaning you seek
only comes to you

when a wound
becomes a window,

when a bridge is built
with the stones of a wall,

when grief is gathered
and spoken in words,

when your lost days
are found alive and well in others,

when poverty is looked upon
and prophecy contemplated.

Sunday Morning

'Consider the office of consoler which Christ our Lord carries out, and compare it with the way friends console one another.' (224)

On Sunday morning
the disciples were locked in
with no way out.
Fear of the Jews,
betrayal of a friend,
the failure of the plan,
inexorable death …
these choked their breath,
paralyzed their limbs,
and held their life captive
like a tombstone.

On Sunday morning
the disciples were locked up
with no way in.
Jesus made himself present
and opened wide
their fear to joy,
their treachery to encounter,
their failure to community,
and death to life.

On Sunday morning
the disciples were so locked in
that no one could enter,
nor could they go out of themselves.
Jesus tore off the bolts
of the door and the spirit.
With the light of the resurrection
they opened up to one another
and in front of the community of witnesses
the whole of Jerusalem,
locked on orders of the Sanhedrin
and with imperial seals,
was opened up to new life.

Free Us, Lord, from Sadness

'Consider the office of consoler which Christ our Lord carries out.' (224)

Free us, Lord, from sadness.
It flows from old wounds
and from sudden, fresh injuries,
neither
fully grieved
for what they cost,
nor properly embraced
for the new freedom they bring.

It seeps in with crafty intent
and snuffs out the shimmer
of the everyday world.
It lays down
its rigidity and torpor
in the joints of bones.
An ungraspable mood
marinates bright memories
in indecipherable blandness.
Yesterday's warm certainties
seem like someone else's archaeology,
anonymous sculptures
in forgotten squares.
Like a cloud pushed by the wind
into monstrous, changing forms,
it conceals the horizon from us
with its ghostly menace.

Sadness hides
behind duty done
and the answer people were expecting.

It adorns its face
with the wrinkles of fasting.
It cloaks itself with a level-headedness
which has everything sorted.
It bends double
with the broad scapular
of the 'humble confrères'
who have seen it all and know it all
and no longer expect anything new
worth the bother of celebrating.

When youthful figures pass by
with their Technicolor laughs,
they leave a sediment of nostalgia,
of chances never taken,
in a fist grown weak.
Sadness leaves in the soul
a residue of dead-beat life,
of the catechism-God
with questions and answers
already learnt by rote,
repeated *ad nauseam*.
Free us from sadness,
Lord of joy!

Nobody Rises Alone

'... the grace to be glad and rejoice intensely because of the great glory and joy of Christ our Lord.' (221)

In the peace that steeps my body
from my back pressed against the ground,
will I let myself be remade by You?
Everything here is reborn from the earth!
The red flowers of the flame trees
and the bright stab of the palms!
Mingle me with the breeze and the sun,
with blue and evening.
I am surrounded by sea
and there are no boats in my harbour!
My ghosts have gone out for the night
from the dungeons of my castle.
Would that I might know you here,
in the silence of the night,
in the absence
which lets me grow alone
out of the hushed sepulchre.
Surely, nobody rises alone.
To rise from deeper down,
to rise from more dead.

CONTEMPLATION TO ATTAIN THE LOVE OF GOD

'... to ask for interior knowledge of all the great good I have received, in order that, stirred to profound gratitude, I may become able to love and serve the Divine Majesty in all things.' (233)

'To love and serve ... in all things': this is the point to which the Exercises have been leading. We have discovered the active presence of God in all reality, whether in social or personal situations. So now we do not have to shut our eyes to find God but rather open them wide to see in the depths of all reality the current of eternal life which courses through the centre.

In the intimacy of 'shut eyes', where we experience interior knowledge of the Lord, just as in the exteriority of 'opened eyes', where we can experience how He creates His Kingdom, it is possible to find God and His action in the world. His active presence is the thread of eternity upon which God is continually hanging our moments, keeping them for ever, regardless of how fleeting they seem to us.

God acts in history with the discretion of a humble servant. This is why we explicitly need this contemplation to 'look' to see how God is present in His creatures, how He gives them to us and how He desires to enter into communion with us without any trace of reticence or gap.

If we do not see in ourselves the gifts that God has given, however limited they may be, then we are unable to rise to great heights of gratitude to the source of these gifts, to the love without measure. We can only feel unlimited in communion with the Unlimited. This is the only path of joy for people who feel their lives are being destroyed and growing weak, and their strength being unaccountably lost in the mystery of God. We are not made for accumulation, perfection or security, which only swell a false and measured 'I', but rather for communion with God, who loves us beyond all measure.

The Gaze of the Sea

'I will consider how God dwells in creatures; in the elements, giving them existence, in the plants, giving them life; in the animals, giving them sensation; in human beings, giving them intelligence ....' (235)

I walked along the edge
of the sea, its waves
breaking raucously
on whetted corals.

Fantasies that go
to my core
hurriedly possessed me,
my senses blocked,
not contemplating the joy
of the cosmos with its speech
of colour and motion.

But, coming back,
I found the sea
within me.
It had looked upon me,
and imbued my intimate repose
with azure peace.
And the palms, too,
were playing
in my corners,
with their green dance
of splintered brightness
in the edges of their fronds.
And with liniment
of iodine and salt
on its fingertips,
the breeze was silently
healing wounds.

And the whole cosmos
desired to make me live again,
right to the marrow of my bones.

And I did not even notice it,
discreet God
of the humble
sacraments!

Your Grace Is Enough for Us

'Take, Lord, and receive all my liberty, my memory, my understanding, and all my will—all that I have and possess. You, Lord, have given all that to me. I now give it back to you, O Lord. All of it is yours. Dispose of it according to your will. Give me love of yourself along with your grace, for that is enough for me.' (234)

I cannot wear you down
with stubborn arguments
or compulsive prayers
to make you grant me
health to serve you,
a long life to do more things,
honour to find
open doors,
or copious resources
to be more effective.

Nor can I ask
for sufferings,
trumpeting my strengths,
as if you needed
a quota of pain
to grant us
what we need.

I only want to ask of you
what you always offer me:
your love and your grace,
which beget life
but can lead to death, too,
in defence of the besieged;
which foster health
but can jeopardise it
in the service of the weak;
which make us loveable,
but can stigmatize us
by not moulding us to the laws;
which make the earth abundant
with all the goods we need,
but might leave us destitute
to make us brothers and sisters
to the outcasts of your world.

I only want to ask you
for your love and your grace,
that I should welcome them in me
as the final truth,
and that my heart say
'it is enough for me'. (234)

Open Heart

'Love consists in a mutual communication between the two persons.' (231)

Will your heart be
an attic of memories
where dated fashions
gather dust?

Will your heart be
a metal filing cabinet
of names and dates
to be plundered efficiently?

Will your heart be
the flower-decked tomb
of dazzling successes,
now dead and buried?

Will your heart be
a museum display-case
to keep you in the rapture
of what you created yesterday?

Or will your heart be
welcome
beat after beat,
a silence which sounds
the embryo of tomorrow,
a detector of the absolute
amidst passing lights,
a fire where
the word, still crisp, is born,
an ample lap
to nourish
the fledgling future?

Freedom Asking

'... to ask for interior knowledge of all the great goods I have received ....' (233)

How will we ever thank you
if we cannot know
all that we have received?

Why did you choose me to exist
among infinite possible creatures?

Who will be able to catalogue
all you give us in just one second?

Whose were the hands and weariness
that surfaced the road I am walking on?

How many times in the darkness
did you hold my life back from the edge of the abyss?

How does the eternal life within me
already infuse with infinity my everyday moments?

If each one of us is a gift for all the others,
will it suffice if I alone intone my song?

Will only the risen Jesus be able to give you thanks
and the rest of us join in his song of praise?

In All Things

'... to love and serve ... in all things.' (233)

To contemplate you in all things
because you instil in all of them
that ultimate, inner energy
which comprises all things;

to discover you in all things,
perforating the shell,
be it beautiful or spoiled,
of all that lives;

to herald you in all things,
close and unknown,
auspicious future
rising from the abyss;

to suffer you in all things,
united with us in the loss
that hurts every creature
and pierces your side;

to love you in all things,
intimate and universal God,
in moving embrace
and in cosmic communion;

to serve you in all things,
toiling towards that
assured, impossible summation in you
of all that exists.

The Unsayable

'Love ought to manifest itself more by deeds than by words.' (230)

It does not matter
that the unsayable
cannot be said
in that endless horizon
where words
surge forward.
It crosses the streets
in frequent transit,
brief gusts
to stop our footsteps
from straying on the asphalt.
The butterfly
takes to the air with it
as it passes by,
a cloud of colours, so elusive.
It sketches the smile
that's born in the eyes
and ends in a hug.
Only once
was the unsayable
made word,
entire eternity
in flesh that fades.
Ever after
an impossible dream
agitates every letter.
It does not matter.
The unsayable
already peeps out,
watching discreetly,
in every attempt
to express it.

A Future So Present

'... to offer and give to the Divine Majesty ... all my possessions, and myself along with them.' (234)

No longer will I ask:

>   when your day will dawn,
>   but where you are breaking through into the present;
>
>   why the evildoer exists,
>   but how you are working out his salvation now;
>
>   when my wound will clear up,
>   but how you are healing it already;
>
>   when wars will end,
>   but where you are building justice;
>
>   when we will be a multitude,
>   but where is today's cave of Bethlehem;
>
>   when oppression will cease,
>   but how to get through the cracks in the system;
>
>   when you will reveal yourself,
>   but where you are hiding.

Because your future is now,
is this universal instant
in which every created thing moves forward
within this mystery of yours we share!

God, Our Servant

'... he, the same Lord, desires to give me even his very self ....' (234)

I praise you, Lord,
our servant,
in all that is created.

> You orchestrate the song of the cosmos
> and sharpen the listening ear.
> You purify the polluted air
> and open the breathing lung.
> You liquefy the body's blood
> and channel the guiding vein.
> You awaken greenness in the leaf
> and give joy to the gazing eye.

I praise you, Lord,
our servant,
in all that is created.

> You impel us towards others
> and beguile us from inside other selves.
> You inspire us in constant encounter,
> disclosing yourself afresh each day.
> You bid us serve the people,
> and in their midst it is us you care for.
> Through love you bestow life on us in every beginning,
> and in love you embrace us at our end.

I praise you, Lord,
our servant,
in all that is created.

> In your fondness for us,
> in your sleepless presence,
> you go from the furrow to the ear of corn
> and from bread to the feast;
> in the day you wander the streets
> and at night you open the door to us;
> in the learned you tell us truths
> and in the lowliest you impart your very self.

I praise you, Lord,
our servant,
in all that is created.

God Always Lesser

'I will consider how God dwells in creatures ....' (235)

I know that you are
the ever greater God.
We name you
the Ineffable,
the Unlimited,
the Incommensurable,
the Infinite:
a kneeling confession
at the utmost of our efforts,
for we cannot
encapsulate you
in a word
nor confine you
to a plan.

Today I prefer to call you
God always lesser.
You are at the far end
of the microscope's
round eye,
on its endless voyage
to the interior
of all that is small.

You are the God
of those three
ellipsis dots
when heart
and dictionary
peter out.

You are the God
of primal complicity,
of two eyes seeking each other
in meeting
without realising,
and of the seminal starting point
in the imagination

and on canvas,
in womb
and furrow.

You are the God
without room,
expelled to the Styx
where the street names
run out,
where, among the refuse,
you bet on life,
where you open your arms
to death,
where life
is so close to
suffering,
and birth
so close to sunset.

Tiny God,
God of below,
I like it
when you startle me,
wrapped in mundane clothes,
when we do not notice you
because we are travelling
in an armoured car
with no windows,
towards what we call
routine,
custom,
the known,
the archived.

Not God Alone

'I will consider how God labors and works for me in all the creatures on the face of the earth ....' (236)

'God alone is enough',
but a God
for whom being alone
in all the universe
is not enough.

God draws near to us
in every being in the world,
which is for us
home, nourishment,
undertaking and horizon.
Cosmic communion
which makes us one with God
in the life that fills us
through the senses,
his gift and presence
in us beyond measure!

Our God,
in the communion
that takes shape in all,
with neither rest nor anything to spare,
in the mothering womb
of breathless history.

God free and unique,
in the innermost nook
of hushed intimacy
where every person
becomes coherent.

Eclipsed God,
of whom all we can hang on to
are his traces,
as frail as the breath
of a marginal child
or as mighty as an earthquake
ripping asunder soul
and empires.

Face-to-face God,
transfigured
in an instant,
when everything else
is lit up from within
in its truth
or vanishes empty
in appearance.

'God alone is enough',
but a God
for whom being alone
in all the universe
is not enough.

In Your Beauty

'I will consider how all good things and gifts descend from above ....' (237)

You have adorned every corner
of our earth-home
with a word of beauty
renewed each day.

In your infinite imagination
you rehearse the rhythms and colours,
the perfumes and patterns,
in which you draw near to us
in the humble sacrament
of passing beauties.

You are love.
Love creates the beautiful.
When it is born in a heart,
glows in the eyes,
enflames the cheeks,
each step,
garlanded with fabrics and songs,
music and perfumes,
insinuates a dance.
Your love has no end,
like the unutterable beauty
which overruns the paintbrush,
the word and the caress.

In beings without charm,
the eye of love
discerns a beauty
locked away from the cameras
of the official competitions.

Like the canvas of an old master
slashed through with a knife,
your comeliness has been marred by us
by municipal overcrowding,
by the desecration of bodies
obliged to rent themselves out,
by the craving of huge eyes

which hack through children like bones.
But your love crucified
with the dreadfulness of blood
transfigures them into light
of dignity and protest,
of prophecy and dance.

All of us seek you
when we want to capture forever
in canvas, ceramic and stone
the beautiful moment
before it fades away.
All of us seek you,
God hidden in the intimacy
of the beings that you illuminate,
for a communion of eternity
which inspires our earthly journey.

Indwelling

'I will consider how God dwells in ... me ... since I am created as a likeness and image of the Divine Majesty.' (235)

Every one of my seconds
sips of your timelessness.

Every one of my spaces
is skin of your open palm.

In the breeze, I inhale
the breath you breathe out.

With finger and thumb
you seal the walls of my wound.

I dip the paintbrush of my inventiveness
in the palette of your fantasy.

Your resurrection courses through
my atoms, hollows and desires.

My creed is of last things,
of bones, of questions.

In your mystery I live
like the witness in the light!

In my mystery you live
like the light in the witness!

Behind the Surface

'... making me his temple, since I am created as a likeness and image of the Divine Majesty.' (235)

We can clasp
thousands of hands
and still be alone,
beset with sensation
in the surface of the skin,
just one hand
and feel in it
the warmth of the absolute.

We can roam
many roads
and still have no future,
the soles of our feet
thick with the miles,
yet take
one single step
and know in it already
the delight of our arriving.

We can gaze
at many landscapes
and still be empty,
resplendent with images
in the paint's skin,
yet contemplate
one lone horizon
and find pictured in it
the fullness of the unbounded.